SKILLS & VALUES:
THE FIRST AMENDMENT

LEXISNEXIS LAW SCHOOL PUBLISHING ADVISORY BOARD

William D. Araiza
Professor of Law
Brooklyn Law School

Lenni B. Benson
Professor of Law
& Associate Dean for Professional Development
New York Law School

Raj Bhala
Rice Distinguished Professor
University of Kansas, School of Law

Ruth Colker
Distinguished University Professor
& Heck-Faust Memorial Chair in Constitutional Law
Ohio State University, Moritz College of Law

Richard D. Freer
Robert Howell Hall Professor of Law
Emory University School of Law

David Gamage
Assistant Professor of Law
UC Berkeley School of Law

Craig Joyce
Andrews Kurth Professor of Law &
Co-Director, Institute for Intellectual Property
and Information Law
University of Houston Law Center

Ellen S. Podgor
Professor of Law & Associate Dean of Faculty Development
and Electronic Education
Stetson University College of Law

David I. C. Thomson
LP Professor & Director, Lawyering Process Program
University of Denver, Sturm College of Law

SKILLS & VALUES: THE FIRST AMENDMENT

Kathleen A. Bergin
Professor of Law
South Texas College of Law

Charles W. "Rocky" Rhodes
Godwin Ronquillo PC Research Professor
and Professor of Law
South Texas College of Law

Library of Congress Cataloging-in-Publication Data

Bergin, Kathleen A.
　Skills & values. The First Amendment / Kathleen A. Bergin, Charles W. Rocky Rhodes.
　　p. cm.
　Includes index.
　ISBN 978-1-4224-2145-1 (soft cover)
　1. United States. Constitution. 1st Amendment. 2. Freedom of speech--United States. 3. Freedom of the press--United States. I. Title. II. Title: First Amendment. III. Title: Skills and values.
　KF4770.B39 2010
　342.7308'52--dc22
　　　　　　　　　　　　　　　　　　　　　　　　　　　2009047056

This publication is designed to provide accurate and authoritative information in regard to the subject matter covered. It is sold with the understanding that the publisher is not engaged in rendering legal, accounting, or other professional services. If legal advice or other expert assistance is required, the services of a competent professional should be sought.

LexisNexis, the knowledge burst logo, and Michie are trademarks of Reed Elsevier Properties Inc, used under license. Matthew Bender is a registered trademark of Matthew Bender Properties Inc.

Copyright © 2010 Matthew Bender & Company, Inc., a member of the LexisNexis Group. All Rights Reserved.

No copyright is claimed in the text of statutes, regulations, and excerpts from court opinions quoted within this work. Permission to copy material exceeding fair use, 17 U.S.C. § 107, may be licensed for a fee of 25¢ per page per copy from the Copyright Clearance Center, 222 Rosewood Drive, Danvers, Mass. 01923, telephone (978) 750-8400.

NOTE TO USERS
To ensure that you are using the latest materials available in this area, please be sure to periodically check the LexisNexis Law School web site for downloadable updates and supplements at www.lexisnexis.com/lawschool.

Editorial Offices
121 Chanlon Road, New Providence, NJ 07974
201 Mission St., San Francisco, CA 94105-1831 (415) 908-3200
www.lexisnexis.com

Preface

This book allows you to experience the connection between theory, doctrine, and practice in First Amendment law. The exercises provide an opportunity for studying First Amendment concepts from the perspective of a practicing attorney who must not only know the law, but also employ lawyering skills and values — such as legal strategy, factual development, advocacy, counseling, drafting, problem solving, and ethical principles — in zealously representing a client.

Each chapter addresses a specific topic covered in most First Amendment law school courses. The chapters begin with an introduction that helps bridge the gap between the actual practice of law and the doctrine and theory you studied in class. You will then have an opportunity to engage in active, "hands on" learning by working through a stand-alone exercise that simulates a real-life legal dilemma. The exercises are as authentic as possible, incorporating materials such as legal pleadings, motions, correspondence, judicial opinions, statutes, discovery materials, and deposition excerpts. Each exercise explains your role, lists the tasks you are required to perform, details the practice skills needed, provides an estimated completion time, has a level of difficulty based on a scale of 1 to 5, and contains pertinent statutes or regulations. Some exercises also include practice tips that highlight important issues or litigation strategies a competent First Amendment lawyer would want to consider.

The book can be used in a number of different ways. Your professor might ask you to complete the tasks in each exercise and produce the assigned written documents for a grade or constructive feedback. Depending on the size and structure of the class, the book might alternatively be used for in-class exercises that you are instructed to complete individually or as part of a group. You can also use the book on your own to reinforce substantive lessons from class and hone important practice skills.

However you use the book, the self-assessment tool included at the end of each chapter suggests ways that a practicing attorney might have approached each exercise. It is not meant to provide "the answer," but to identify issues and strategies you should have considered in order to effectively represent your client. Indeed, you may come up with alternative yet equally effective ways of addressing your client's needs. For this reason, you should approach the self-assessment tool as a template for further discussion, rather than an all-encompassing answer to the problem at hand. Just be sure that you do not view the self-assessment tool until after you complete the exercise on your own or as it is assigned by your professor — after all, there is no "self-assessment tool" when you are in practice!

You may also want to use the LexisNexis Web Course that was created for this book, which contains forms to assist you in completing some of the exercises, audio and video files, links to some of the key cases, and other supplemental materials designed to increase your understanding of both doctrine and practice. We hope that you find both the book and the platform enjoyable and useful to your development of lawyering skills and values.

Kathleen Bergin
Charles W. "Rocky" Rhodes
Houston, Texas

Table of Contents

Chapter One: **Incitement of Illegal Activity............ 1**

    Exercise 1..3
    Self-Assessment......................................10

Chapter Two: **Obscenity and Sexually Explicit Material........................... 15**

    Exercise 2..17
    Self-Assessment......................................26

Chapter Three: **The Fighting Words Doctrine 29**

    Exercise 3..32
    Self-Assessment......................................34

Chapter Four: **Commercial Speech.................. 37**

    Exercise 4..39
    Self-Assessment......................................44

Chapter Five: **Time, Place and Manner Restrictions ... 51**

    Exercise 5..53
    Self-Assessment......................................58

Chapter Six: **Public Employee Speech Rights 63**

    Exercise 6..65
    Self-Assessment......................................68

Chapter Seven: **Public School Students' Speech Rights....................... 73**

    Exercise 7..75
    Self-Assessment......................................80

Chapter Eight: **Government Speech................. 83**

    Exercise 8..85
    Self-Assessment......................................88

Chapter Nine: Freedom of Expressive Association 91

Exercise 9. 93
Self-Assessment. 100

Chapter Ten: The Political Process and the First Amendment 103

Exercise 10. 105
Self-Assessment. 108

Chapter Eleven: The Newsgathering Function and Freedom of the Press. 113

Exercise 11. 115
Self-Assessment. 121

Chapter Twelve: The Establishment Clause. 127

Exercise 12. 129
Self-Assessment. 132

Chapter Thirteen: The Free Exercise Clause 135

Exercise 13. 138
Self-Assessment Part I 148
Self-Assessment Part II. 150

Chapter Fourteen: Vagueness and Overbreadth 151

Exercise 14. 153
Self-Assessment. 158

Chapter 1
INCITEMENT OF ILLEGAL ACTIVITY

INTRODUCTION

The cases addressing incitement of illegal activity usually arise in one of three situations. First, sometimes a prosecution is based on speech or symbolic expression made by a "rabble rouser" in public who is trying to whip a crowd into a frenzy to engage in some illegal activity. This has occasionally arisen in the context of a group embracing racial superiority principles, such as the Aryan Nations or the Ku Klux Klan. It has also occurred in protests that started peaceably, but then a protestor or group of protestors encouraged others to engage in illegal activities, including assaults, trespass, or property destruction. These cases typically reach an attorney after an arrest of the rabble rouser who then must be prosecuted or defended.

The second situation involves more surreptitious activities, in which an organization attempts to develop subversive plans in secret. This may occur with an anarchist or terrorist group that has designs to overthrow the government of the United States. For instance, after the 9/11 attacks, the government claims groups of radical jihadists met secretly in the United States to recruit members and raise funds to join with foreign terrorist organizations in launching attacks against the United States. During the Cold War, there were similar contentions that groups of Communists were secretly spreading Marxist dogma that would then be used at the appropriate time to overthrow the government of the United States. Due to the secrecy of these organizations and their violent objectives, the government sometimes is faced with a dilemma — either move in quickly and face the risk that only abstract teaching protected by the First Amendment rather than unprotected preparation for violent action has occurred, or wait and face the risk that the organization may accomplish its objectives.

The final scenario involves the publication or dissemination of materials that either contain or depict romanticism of violence or instructions for committing unlawful acts. The key question in these cases is the speaker's intent. A song, for example, may praise the virtues of suicide, or the thrill of killing a police officer, but if the performer did not intend that the viewers or listeners commit an act of violence, it is protected under the First Amendment. This protection is lost only in those rare situations in which the performer or publisher has an intent to incite the audience into likely, imminent unlawful acts, such as providing detailed instructions in seminars on filing fraudulent income tax returns, *see, e.g., United States v. Schiff*, 379 F.3d 621, 629 (9th Cir. 2004), or selling detailed instructions on making illegal drugs or becoming an assassin. *See, e.g., Rice v. Palladin Enterprises, Inc.*, 128 F.3d 233, 243–50 (4th Cir. 1997).

The Supreme Court pronounced the governing standard for incitement of illegal activity in *Bradenburg v. Ohio*, 395 U.S. 444 (1969). The Court explained that the government may not "forbid or proscribe advocacy of the use of force or of law violation except where such advocacy is directed to inciting or producing imminent lawless action and is likely to produce such action." *Id.* at 447. But while the test is easy to state, it is often more difficult to apply.

EXERCISE 1:

You are a United States Attorney working with the Federal Bureau of Investigation regarding an ongoing investigation of Ali Laden, a United States citizen living in Alexandria, Virginia who is under surveillance due to his suspected links to the terrorist organization al Qaeda. The FBI wants you to prosecute Ali Laden for treason if doing so would not violate the First Amendment.

The FBI periodically brings you the information it has obtained through public records and through an informant regarding Ali Laden's activities in the days following September 11, 2001. The FBI then wants you to prepare an indictment (which is similar to a complaint in a civil case) against Ali Laden for treason, if there is sufficient information to establish probable cause. The Bureau also wants your written opinion regarding whether Ali Laden's activities are protected by the First Amendment and whether the arrest should be delayed to obtain more evidence.

Required Tasks for Each Blog Entry or Report:

Task 1: Prepare an indictment for treason if sufficient information exists to do so in compliance with a prosecutor's ethical obligations under Rule 3.8 of the Model Rules of Professional Conduct (the LexisNexis Web Course contains a form for the indictment that has been started for you, and there is a completed indictment that you may review in Exercise 9).

Task 2: Prepare a memo on whether Ali Laden's activities are protected by the First Amendment.

Task 3: Advise in your memo whether the arrest should be delayed to obtain more evidence.

Practice Skills Utilized:

Skill 1: Constitutional and statutory analysis
Skill 2: Critical reasoning from cases
Skill 3: Criminal pleading
Skill 4: Strategic thinking

Estimated Time for Completion: Approximately 1 hour per entry

Level of Difficulty (1 to 5):

Pertinent Constitutional and Statutory Provisions:

> United States Constitution Article III, § 3:
>
>> Treason against the United States, shall consist only in levying War against them, or in adhering to their Enemies, giving them Aid and Comfort. No Person shall be convicted of Treason unless on the Testimony of two Witnesses to the same overt Act, or on Confession in open Court.
>
> 18 U.S.C. § 2381: Treason
>
>> Whoever, owing allegiance to the United States, levies war against them or adheres to their enemies, giving them aid and comfort within the United States or elsewhere, is guilty of treason and shall suffer death, or shall be imprisoned not less than five years and fined under this title but not less than $10,000, and shall be incapable of holding any office under the United States.

Practice Tip: After carefully analyzing the constitutional and statutory elements of treason, you may want to supplement your understanding with case law research. You also will need to pay careful attention to how to prove all these elements, especially considering the need for testimony from two witnesses to the same overt act.

www.laden.com.blogspot   9/12/01

ALI LADEN
FOUNDER
THE CENTER FOR ISLAMIC INFORMATION

Praise to Allah!

Yesterday, the World witnessed the deserved retribution against America for its crimes against our way of life!

Upon hearing the news of the destruction of the two towers of the World Trade Center yesterday, my heart felt good omens that I had to spread to my brothers. This is a strong signal that Western supremacy (especially that of America) is coming to a quick end, God Willing, as occurred to these buildings.

The attacks yesterday were justified under our fatwas. Their success indicates that the End of Time battle has begun. Be prepared in spirit for this new struggle!

Join me tonight at the Center as I discuss these events and how the End of Time battle has been foretold!

The Exercise:

The FBI Informant reveals that Ali Laden was joined by three dozen followers that night at the Center. During the meeting, he described the sacred religious rulings, or fatwas, that he believed justified the 9/11 attacks, and then he ended with the following prayer:

> Oh, Allah, destroy America. Slay the unbelievers wherever you find them. Let death come to them by the hands of the holy fighters. And help more to answer the call to this fight.

Complete the assigned tasks based on Ali Laden's 9/12/01 conduct.

www.laden.com.blogspot   9/13/01

ALI LADEN
FOUNDER
THE CENTER FOR ISLAMIC INFORMATION

The first stages of jihad are upon us. The Western world, including America, should be stabbed until it bleeds to death.

The Taliban in Afghanistan is preparing for an assault by the infidels. They need our support and our prayers. They need holy fighters to prevail in this jihad.

Join me tonight at the Center to pray for victory in this struggle!

The Exercise:

At the Center that night, the FBI informant explains that Ali Laden was joined by approximately a dozen of his followers. Most of the meeting consisted of prayers and the recitation of verses and religious rulings that Ali Laden believed justified jihad.

After the meeting concluded, Ali Laden approached six of his followers individually. He asked them to join with him the next night at his home for further study of the justness of the cause. The informant was one of the six who was invited to Ali Laden's home.

Complete the assigned tasks based on Ali Laden's 9/13/01 conduct.

Transcript of Informant's 9/14/01 Report on Ali Laden

I went to Ali Laden's house about 7 p.m. As I approached, I noticed that the house was entirely dark, with all the shades pulled down. I knocked on the door, and then it was opened. Four people were inside, including Ali Laden. The room was illuminated only by a few candles. Ali Laden then approached me and asked for my cell phone, which I handed to him.

Another two people came to the door shortly thereafter. Ali Laden asked for their cell phones as well, which they handed over. He then placed all the cell phones in a small lock box in the entry way, and had us walk with him into the living area of his home.

He began by stating that we were all alone, cut off from the outside world. No cell phones, no electricity — he had even cut the phone lines to his house. He needed our meeting to be as secretive as possible due to its great urgency.

He said he wanted us to travel abroad and join the Taliban in fighting against the American troops. Of all of his followers, he believed we were the most worthy, and we would obtain salvation by fighting in the jihad. He asked each of us if we would agree to do so. All six of us agreed. He told us to return tomorrow evening and he would provide us with instructions on how to travel to Pakistan and join al Qaeda without being detected by the authorities.

The Exercise:

After showing you this transcript, the FBI wants you to complete the assigned tasks for 9/14/01.

Transcript of Informant's 9/15 Report on Ali Laden

I returned to Ali Laden's house this evening at 7 p.m. Everything was the same as the night before — the house was dark, Ali Laden collected all the cell phones, and we joined in his living room.

But on this occasion it was all business. Ali Laden had prepared detailed instructions regarding how we each should proceed to join the Taliban. The instructions explained step-by-step how to obtain the travel visas that we would need to get to Pakistan and what to say when we were asked the purpose of our travel.

Ali Laden said that, after we obtained the travel visas, we should travel by train to New York City. From there we should fly to Pakistan. Once we got to Pakistan, an Al Qaeda operative would meet us and then escort us to Afghanistan to assist the Taliban cause against the United States.

The Exercise:

Complete the assigned tasks for 9/15/01.

**DO NOT PROCEED TO THE NEXT PAGE UNTIL YOU
HAVE COMPLETED THE EXERCISE**

SELF-ASSESSMENT

Required Tasks for Each Entry:

Task 1: Prepare an indictment for treason if sufficient information exists to do so in compliance with a prosecutor's ethical obligations under Rule 3.8 of the Model Rules of Professional Conduct.

Task 2: Prepare a memo on whether Ali Laden's activities are protected by the First Amendment.

Task 3: Advise in your memo whether the arrest should be delayed to obtain more evidence.

Practice Skills Utilized:

Skill 1: Constitutional and statutory analysis

Skill 2: Critical reasoning from cases

Skill 3: Criminal pleading

Skill 4: Strategic thinking

Task 1: **Prepare an indictment for treason if sufficient information exists to do so in compliance with a prosecutor's ethical obligations.**

Analysis of Treason: The first step is to ensure that you understand the elements of the crime of treason. Under the relevant constitutional and statutory provisions, treason requires levying war against the United States, or in "adhering to their Enemies, giving them Aid and Comfort." Treason also requires the testimony of two witnesses to the same overt act or a confession in open court.

Case Research: Frequently, you may need to supplement the statutory elements with case law research. What constitutes "adhering to their Enemies" and "Aid and Comfort"? The United States Supreme Court has concluded that it requires a subjective intent to betray the United States that objectively provides aid and comfort to the enemy. *Cramer v. United States*, 325 U.S. 1, 29 (1945). If a citizen favors the enemy, but does not commit an act providing any aid, treason cannot be established. On the other hand, even actions that assist the enemy cannot constitute treason unless there is an intent to betray the United States.

Critical Reasoning: A prosecutor is ethically committed to serving justice by refraining, among other obligations, from prosecuting or threatening to prosecute a charge that the prosecutor knows is not supported by probable cause. *See* Rule 3.8 (a) of the Model Rules of Professional Conduct. Thus, you should not proceed with an indictment to the grand jury in the absence of your own belief that probable cause exists. Under this standard, when did Ali Laden's activities become treasonous? Although he may have had the intent from 9/12/01 to betray the United States, evidenced by his expressed desire to destroy America and support the holy fighters, at what point did his actions objectively provide aid and comfort to the enemy?

Treason convictions were upheld after World War II for Americans who worked with and were paid by the Axis powers for broadcasting propaganda to try to interfere with the American war effort. *See D'Aquino v. United States*, 192 F.2d 338 (9th Cir. 1951); *Gillars v. United States*, 182 F.2d 962 (D.C. Cir. 1950); *Chandler v. United States*, 171 F.2d 921 (1st Cir. 1948). Would the same rationale apply to Ali Laden's 9/12 and 9/13 blog postings and statements during the meetings justifying an attack, requesting support for its principles, and praying for the destruction of America by holy fighters? Or is there a difference because there is no evidence at this juncture that Ali Laden is being paid or is coordinating his postings with the enemy?

Is Ali Laden's 9/13 request for a meeting with some of his followers at his house an action providing aid and comfort to the enemy? Until the topic of the meeting is known, could this request tend to provide the enemy any aid?

If the postings and meetings at the Center are not sufficient for treason, could treason be established during the first meeting on 9/14 when Ali Laden obtains the agreement of the six individuals to travel abroad and join the Taliban? Here, this agreement does seem to provide "aid and comfort" to the enemy. It is not necessary that the treasonous plan succeeds as long as the acts tend to strengthen the enemy or are efforts to assist the enemy. *See Haupt v. United States*, 330 U.S. 631, 644 (1947).

	The meeting on 9/15 undoubtedly supports a treason charge. Ali Laden indicates that he is communicating with the enemy and is making detailed arrangements for six of his followers to join the fight. This arguably even satisfies the standard for "levying war" on the United States.
Pleading:	For each of the entries that you believe constitute treason, you will need to draft an indictment. The indictment will need to have a caption identifying the parties to the case (the United States and Ali Laden), a title, and factual and legal allegations sufficient to constitute the crime of treason, as outlined above. The template on the LexisNexis Web Course should have assisted you in starting the drafting process.
Task 2:	**Prepare a memo on whether Ali Laden's activities are protected by the First Amendment.**
Case Analysis:	Under the *Brandenburg* test, the government may not criminalize advocating the use of force or unlawful conduct "except where such advocacy is directed to inciting or producing imminent lawless action and is likely to produce such action." The mere teaching of the moral necessity of a resort to force and violence is not the same as preparing a group for violent action and steering it to such action. *Noto v. United States*, 367 U.S. 290, 297–99 (1961).
Critical Reasoning:	When did Ali Laden cross the line between teaching the moral necessity of jihad and preparing a group for violent action? The 9/12 blog post and the subsequent meeting presumably were only teaching and requesting prayers for support of the jihad. The 9/13 blog post and meeting, although more incendiary, probably also involved mere teaching. Notice that even the 9/13 request for the followers to join him the next night only mentioned further study of the justness of the cause rather than any type of preparation for violent action.
	The 9/14 meeting appears to have started the preparation for violent action. Ali Laden obtained the agreement of his followers to travel abroad and to resist the United States. He also stated he would provide them with detailed instructions on how to accomplish these tasks. Thus, there was

an intent to produce imminent lawless action and there was a likelihood that such lawless action would occur soon. This was confirmed by the subsequent meeting on 9/15 which provided the detailed instructions on pursuing this unlawful course of action.

Task 3: **Advise as to whether the arrest should be delayed to obtain more evidence.**

Strategic Thinking: Because the 9/12 and 9/13 postings and meetings did not establish a clear case of treason or indicate that a prosecution would satisfy the strictures of the First Amendment, your advice should have been to wait. To make its case, the FBI needed evidence of an overt act providing aid to the enemy and speech that had gone beyond mere teaching.

The FBI could have arrested Ali Laden after the 9/14 meeting. The issue on 9/14 is whether it was preferable to wait for more information. Although Ali Laden had obtained the agreement from the six followers to travel abroad and join the fight, and he had agreed to provide them detailed instructions the next evening, an arrest at that juncture would not have provided the FBI as much information regarding the particulars of the plot. This information could be useful to help guard against similar attempts in the future. There is also a concern that on 9/14 it may be difficult to obtain the testimony of a second witness (other than the informant) to an overt act.

After the 9/15 meeting, the FBI has more information, and may even be able to catch some of the followers in the act of trying to obtain travel visas, etc. This would assist in meeting the constitutional and statutory requirement of two witnesses to the overt act supporting the treason charge.

Chapter 2
OBSCENITY AND SEXUALLY EXPLICIT MATERIAL

INTRODUCTION

Restrictions on sexually explicit material typically take one of two forms: (1) a flat prohibition on the production, sale, or distribution of obscenity; or (2) the regulation of adult businesses that are sexually explicit though not obscene. Lawmakers are free to restrict or even ban obscenity because it does not qualify as protected speech under the First Amendment. Measures that burden the operation of adult businesses, however, will be subject to intermediate scrutiny under the "secondary effects" doctrine.

Miller v. California, 413 U.S. 15 (1973), defined obscenity as material that depicts or describes "patently offensive" sexual conduct that is specifically set forth by applicable law. The material must both appeal to the "prurient interest" when viewed as a whole by the average person, and lack serious literary, artistic, political, or scientific value. Whether the material is patently offensive and appeals to the prurient interest is judged by a "contemporary community standard." Whether it lacks serious value is judged by a nation-wide reasonable person standard.

In practice, it is sometimes difficult to identify the relevant "community" whose values will determine whether the material is exceedingly prurient or offensive. In *Miller,* the Court rejected a claim of constitutional error based on the prosecution's failure to offer evidence of a national standard, and affirmed the trial court's instructions that the jury consider state-wide attitudes. According to Chief Justice Burger, differences in people's taste and temperament make it impossible to ascertain a uniform national standard of obscenity. Though the First Amendment protects some explicit material, he explained, it does not require "that the people of Maine or Mississippi accept public depictions of conduct found tolerable in Las Vegas, or New York City." *Id.* at 32. This means that what is obscene in one jurisdiction might not be obscene in another.

Application of a state-wide standard is not *required*, however, and later cases made clear that the fact-finder is permitted to "draw on knowledge of the community or vicinage from which [it] comes." *Hamling v. United States*, 418 U.S. 87, 104 (1974). In some cases, a state statute might require that the jury consider the community values of the county or judicial district where the offense is committed. Other statutes might reference a generic "community standard," in which case you may have an opportunity to request jury instructions that clarify the scope of inquiry. In any obscenity case, therefore, a prosecutor can increase the likelihood of conviction by determining which venues are proper, and filing charges in the most conservative one.

Today, of course, most obscene material is distributed over the internet, and courts have split on the issue of whether a national community standard should apply in on-line obscenity cases. *Compare U.S. v. Little*, 2010 U.S. App. LEXIS 2320 *with U.S. v. Kilbride*, 584 F.3d 1240 (2009). The Supreme Court has recognized the right of adults to access on-line content that might be inappropriate for minors, but has not squarely addressed the community standards issue as it relates to the internet. *See ACLU v. Ashcroft*, 535 U.S. 564 (2002); *Reno v. ACLU*, 521 U.S. 844 (1997).

Unlike the first two *Miller* prongs, the third prong relies on a national reasonable person standard to determine whether the material as a whole lacks "serious literary, artistic, political or scientific value." *Pope v. Illinois*, 481 U.S. 497 (1987). On the one hand, this prong expands the scope of the First Amendment by protecting speech that is otherwise prurient or patently offensive under the relevant community standard. On the other hand, only material with *serious* value is protected; prurient and patently offensive material that has *some* social value is still obscene.

The government not only has the power to ban obscenity under *Miller*, it can also restrict the operation of sexually explicit adult businesses under the "secondary effects" doctrine. Measures designed to stabilize property values and reduce the risk of crime and sexually transmitted disease are deemed to be "content neutral" even when they apply to adult businesses exclusively. Under the applicable intermediate scrutiny standard, a city might concentrate adult theaters within a particular geographic location or limit the proximity of one theater to another without violating the First Amendment. *See Renton v. Playtime Theatres*, 475 U.S. 41 (1986). It might even ban one particular form of adult expression, nude dancing for instance, so long as alternative means of communicating the underlying erotic message are available. *See Erie v. Pap's A.M.*, 529 U.S. 277 (2000).

Practice Tip: The Supreme Court has declined to formally expand the "secondary effects" doctrine beyond cases that involve adult entertainment. *See, e.g., Boos v. Barry*, 485 U.S. 312, 320–21 (1988) (declining to extend secondary effects doctrine to ban on picket signs within 500 feet of a foreign embassy). The doctrine has been applied by lower federal courts in other circumstances, however. *See, e.g., Long v. Board of Education of Jefferson County*, 121 F. Supp. 2d 621, 624–25 (W.D. Ky. 2000) (identifying "gang activity" as dangerous secondary effect that justified student dress code).

OBSCENITY AND SEXUALLY EXPLICIT MATERIAL

EXERCISE 2:

Your client, Devon Herschild, is the owner of Rest Easy Hotels. She is served with a summons and criminal complaint that charges her with violating certain provisions of the state code. She wants to know whether the charges are legitimate, and whether she can proceed with plans to open a new hotel in a busy downtown area without violating the law.

Herschild brings you a copy of the charging document, along with a letter she received from Citizens for Community Values. How do you advise her?

Required Tasks:

Task 1: Draft a Motion to Dismiss asserting all appropriate grounds for relief (the LexisNexis Web Course contains a form for the motion that has been started for you).

Task 2: Identify facts that may help or harm your client in a future obscenity prosecution.

Task 3: Provide client advice to mitigate the risk of future litigation.

Practice Skills Utilized:

Skill 1: Statutory analysis and case law research
Skill 2: Motion drafting
Skill 3: Factual development
Skill 4: Creative problem solving

Estimated Time for Completion: Approximately 1 hour

Level of Difficulty (1 to 5):

State of Astoria	District Court
County of New Yonkers	Fifth Judicial District
	Court File No. 742

State of Astoria, [x] Summons [x] Complaint
    Plaintiff,

v.

Devon Herschild (DOB: 11/07/1962)

c/o Rest Easy Hotels

1234 Gateway Lane

New Yonkers, Astoria 01298

    Defendant.

The Complainant, being duly sworn, makes complaint to the above-named Court and states that there is probable cause to believe that the Defendant committed the following offense(s):

	Count 1
Charge:	Prohibition of Public Lewdness and Indecency
Statute:	§11.01 – Public Lewdness
Maximum Sentence:	Fine up to $4,000 OR up to 1 year in jail OR both.
	Count 2
Charge:	Prohibition of Public Lewdness and Indecency
Statute:	§11.02 – Indecent Exposure
Maximum Sentence:	Fine up to $2,000 OR up to 180 days in jail OR both.
	Count 3
Charge:	Prohibition of Obscenity
Statute:	§41.14 – "Contemporary Community Standards" Defined
Maximum Sentence:	None indicated

Statement of Probable Cause

The Defendant is the owner and operator of Rest Easy Hotels, a place of public accommodation licensed to do business in the state of Astoria.

The hotel operates a pay-per-view system through which adult guests can purchase sexually explicit movies that play on television sets provided in their room. On July 14, I, Officer Jennifer Hathaway with the Astoria Police Department, posed as a hotel guest, reserved a room, and used the pay-per-view system to order a sexually explicit movie. The movie ran on the television set in my room, and my account was charged $19.95.

The movie purchased from Rest Easy Hotels was sexually explicit, and qualified as obscene under the above referenced statutes.

Complainant's Name	Complainant's Signature
Officer Jennifer Hathaway City of Astoria Police Department Badge #324	*Jennifer Hathaway*

Being authorized to prosecute the offenses charged, I approve this complaint. Prosecutor's Name: Address: 89 Smithfield Road New Yonkers, Astoria Phone: 888-238-2847 Attorney Registration #: 34879398	Prosecutor's Signature: **Kenneth Jones**

Finding of Probable Cause

From the above sworn facts, and any supporting affidavits or supplemental sworn testimony, I, the Issuing Officer, have determined that probable cause exists to support Defendant's arrest or other lawful steps to secure an appearance in court, or Defendant's detention, if already in custody, pending further proceedings. Defendant is therefore charged with the above-stated offense.

[x] Summons

Therefore, you the above-named Defendant, are hereby summoned to appear on the 5th day of August, at 8:30 am, before the above-named court at 1439 Almaeda Avenue, Astoria, to answer this complaint.

This Complaint, duly subscribed and sworn to, is issued by the undersigned Judicial Officer, this 28th of July.

Judicial Officer

Name: Petra Kovicz, Magistrate

Signature: *Petra Kovicz*

Citizens for Family Values
2005 Heaven's Way
New Yonkers, Astoria 01298

Fifty Years of Caring, Commitment and Community

Devon Herschild
Rest Easy Hotels
1234 Gateway Lane
New Yonkers, Astoria 01298

Dear Ms. Herschild:

Citizens for Family Values demands that Rest Easy Hotels cease offering its guests adult-content pay-per-view movies. These sexually explicit films patently offend Astoria's core community values and violate three separate sections of the state code. Those sections are attached to this correspondence.

We understand that Rest Easy Hotels provides unparalleled service to a world-wide clientele. Your advertisements boast that more than 37,000 guests lodged at your downtown facility last year alone. You also hosted the International Governors Conference at the request of Astoria Governor Karine Johnson, and serviced more than 112 dignitaries from across the globe. The five-star reputation associated with your establishment cannot be sustained long-term if Rest Easy continues to pander offensive hard-core entertainment to guests.

As reported in *The Nation Today* newspaper, other national hotel chains, including Comfort Sleep, Merrylodge, and Milton, have wisely discontinued obscene move entertainment. Experts estimate that adult movies generate $5 million in annual revenue for hotel chains, and attribute 50–60% of pay-per-view revenues to adult products. Yet these businesses have chosen to promote the good morals of the community over immoral profits. We hope these developments inspire you to follow their lead.

Sincerely,

Stanli Grover
Stanli Grover
President, Citizens for Family Values

State of Astoria
Codified Statutes of 1963, Annotated
Prohibition of Public Lewdness and Indecency

§11.01 — Public Lewdness

It shall be unlawful in the State of Astoria to:

1. Knowingly engage in one of the following acts in a public place, OR

2. Engage in one of the following acts while reckless as to whether another is present who will be offended or alarmed:

    a. Act of sexual intercourse,

    b. Act of deviate sexual intercourse,

    c. Act of sexual contact, OR

    d. Act of sexual contact with a bird or animal.

Public Lewdness is a Class A misdemeanor.

Class A misdemeanor: Fine up to $4,000 OR up to 1 year in jail OR both.

Historical Reference: 1992 amendment authorized financial penalty as alternative to jail sentence established by Codified Statutes of 1963.

§11.02 — Indecent Exposure

It shall be unlawful in the State of Astoria for any individual to:

1. Expose themselves with intent to arouse or gratify the sexual desire of any person, AND

2. The individual exposed knows or has reason to know that another is present who will be offended or alarmed.

This is a Class B misdemeanor.

Class B misdemeanor: Fine up to $2,000 OR up to 180 days in jail OR both.

Historical Reference: 1992 amendment authorized financial penalty as alternative to jail sentence established by Codified Statutes of 1963.

OBSCENITY AND SEXUALLY EXPLICIT MATERIAL

State of Astoria
Codified Statutes of 1963, Annotated
Prohibition of Obscenity
Contemporary Community Standards

§41.14 — "Contemporary Community Standards" Defined

a. PURPOSE AND INTENT

It is the purpose of this statute to define the terms 'contemporary standards' and 'contemporary community standards' as that term is used as one element of a definition of obscenity;

It is the further purpose of this statute to provide public and private decision-making bodies with a standard or measure by which to determine what constitutes obscenity within the State of Astoria.

b. STANDARDS

Within the State of Astoria, any business which displays, distributes, or engages in commerce involving representations or descriptions of any of the following, whether involving children or adults: ultimate sexual acts, normal or perverted, actual or simulated; and representations or descriptions of masturbatory, excretory functions, and lewd exhibition of the genitals, is determined to be patently offensive to the adults of the State of Astoria, and should be considered by such employees, agents, representatives and governing bodies to "appeal to the prurient interest." All public and private decision-making bodies or individuals shall recognize this as a standard set by the adults of the State of Astoria to be used in determining whether such business is obscene.

DO NOT PROCEED TO THE NEXT PAGE UNTIL YOU HAVE COMPLETED THE EXERCISE

SELF-ASSESSMENT

Required Tasks

Task 1: Draft a Motion to Dismiss asserting all appropriate grounds for relief.

Task 2: Identify facts that may help or harm your client in a future obscenity prosecution.

Task 3: Provide client advice to mitigate the risk of future litigation.

Practice Skills Utilized

Skill 1: Statutory analysis and case law research

Skill 2: Motion drafting

Skill 3: Factual development

Skill 4: Creative problem solving

Task 1:	**Draft a Motion to Dismiss asserting all appropriate grounds for relief**
Motion Drafting:	Refer to the Skills & Values Exercise 2 on the LexisNexis web course that came with this book: Motion to Dismiss.
Statutory Analysis:	There is no liability under §§ 11.01 and 11.02. These statutes apply to physical conduct, not commercial transactions or depictions of obscenity. The motion to dismiss these two counts is therefore based on the prosecutor's failure to allege legally sufficient facts to support the charges.
Case Research:	There is no liability under § 41.14. The statute defines "contemporary community standards" as a matter of law. *Smith v. United States*, 431 U.S. 291, 303 (1977), reaffirmed that contemporary community standards present a question of fact for the jury that cannot be defined legislatively. The motion to dismiss this count is therefore based on the First Amendment right to freedom of speech.
	Do not assume the validity of legal authority asserted by an adversary. Here, the charging document cited two statutes that by their terms do not apply to your client. The third statute was rendered unconstitutional by *Smith*.
	You may have found §41.14 difficult to decipher. It is an actual ordinance proposed by a municipality in Texas, and modified slightly to fit our setting in Astoria. You will confront many examples of

poor drafting in practice and need to devote the time and patience to work through it. Statutes that are too poorly drafted, however, may be unconstitutionally vague. *See* Chapter 14.

Task 2:

Factual Development:

Facts relevant to future obscenity prosecutions

Statutes: Though §§ 11.01 and 11.02 do not apply to the sale of obscene movies, prohibitions on sexual conduct might be used as evidence of community standards for the jury to consider in an appropriate obscenity case.

Did you account for the following facts that could mitigate the significance of these statutes:

- When they were enacted
- When they were last enforced
- The relevance of the "historical reference"
- Whether there have been successful prosecutions under the ordinances, or simply arrests

Correspondence: The Governor's choice to hold an international conference with dignitary guests at Rest Easy undermines the prosecutor's community standards argument.

Nation Today: Product demand as mentioned in the article could help establish community standards. Did you consider whether out-of-state guests could influence community standards in Astoria? What about the value of national revenue receipts?

Don't forget to use material provided by an adversary to your benefit. The correspondence from Citizens for Family Values and the referenced newspaper article contain information relevant to the question of community standards that may ultimately benefit Rest Easy.

Task 3:

Case Review
Creative
Problem Solving:

Mitigate the risk of future litigation for your client

You might have advised Rest Easy to consider locating its new hotel within an area zoned for adult entertainment. Under *City of Renton v. Playtime Theaters, Inc.*, 475 U.S. 41, 51–52

(1986), lawmakers can zone adult entertainment establishments under the secondary effects doctrine, though by doing so they effectively provide adult businesses a safe haven from prosecution. Rest Easy may nonetheless still face public pressure from influential community groups which may influence its decision to expand.

Chapter 3
THE FIGHTING WORDS DOCTRINE

INTRODUCTION

The First Amendment may provide a defense if your client is charged with a "disorderly conduct" or "breach of the peace" violation. You will first need to determine the basis for the charge. Was your client arrested on account of disagreeable language, or unruly or disruptive conduct that posed a direct threat to public order and safety? An arrest for jumping a subway turnstile or wielding a knife in public hardly raises a legitimate free speech concern. It may be a closer call, however, when the arrest is based on actual speech.

Speech alone can serve as the basis for a valid arrest when it falls into an unprotected category. Such is the case with "fighting words," defined by the Supreme Court as words that by their very utterance inflict injury or tend to provoke an immediate breach of the peace. *Chaplinsky v. New Hampshire*, 315 U.S. 568, 572 (1942). The government is free to regulate fighting words because, in the Court's view, they constitute no essential part of the exposition of ideas.

Whether your client engaged in unprotected fighting words depends on the facts and circumstances of each case. The test is not what a particular addressee thinks, but what people of "common intelligence" think would cause a "reasonable addressee" to fight. Moreover, fighting words must be directed to an intended individual or group or listeners. Consider the use of profanity in *Cohen v. California*, 403 U.S. 15 (1971), where the Supreme Court held that a Vietnam War protestor whose jacket bore the words "fuck the draft" could not be criminally prosecuted for "maliciously and willfully disturbing the peace and quiet." Under the circumstances, Justice Harlan wrote, the expletive was not a "direct personal insult" that was likely to incite a violent response. Nor was the jacket forced upon an unwilling "captive audience." In the Court's view, those offended by the jacket could avoid the insult simply by averting their eyes.

Depending on the circumstances, however, courts might find that profanity is not protected speech. Examples include cases where a defendant cursed at a nude sunbather, displayed a sexually derogatory sign to a motorist, or shouted profanity laced racial slurs to someone waiting at a bus stop. The nature of the inquiry is so fact intensive, however, that disparate results can occur in situations that at first appear quite similar. For instance, a student who gestured a middle finger to school officials was properly convicted of disorderly conduct, whereas a driver who did the same to another motorist was not. *Compare Coggin v. State*, 123 S.W.3d 82 (Tex. App. 2003) *with*

In re S.J.N.-K, 647 N.W. 2d 707 (S.D. 2002). Lawyers must examine the surrounding circumstances carefully, including the frequency, volume, and context of the remarks, to make sense of these outcomes.

Some fighting words situations warrant special consideration. First, police officers might be held to a higher standard of restraint than an average citizen on account of their special skills and training. *See Marttila v. City of Lynchburg*, 535 S.E.2d. 693 (Va. App. 2000). Insults, slurs, and profanity directed to a police officer are therefore less likely to provoke a violent response, and consequently less likely to constitute fighting words, than the same language directed towards an average person. When potential fighting words are directed to a third party, however, the police must make reasonable efforts to control an unruly crowd before arresting the speaker.

Second, even though fighting words are not protected by the First Amendment, content-based measures that prohibit some types of fighting words but not others might trigger strict scrutiny review. Applying that standard, the Supreme Court invalidated an ordinance that punished only fighting words related to race, color, creed, religion or gender, but not fighting words related to other characteristics. *See R.A.V. v. St. Paul*, 505 U.S. 377 (1992). Note the "special virulence" exception, however, which holds that strict scrutiny does not apply when a content-based restriction on a sub-category of speech relates back to the very reason the entire category of speech is unprotected. What does this mean? Well, instead of prohibiting all depictions of obscenity, a state might choose to prohibit only the "most patently offensive" depictions. Strict scrutiny would not apply, as the line between what the state prohibits (the most patently offensive obscenity) and what it allows (less patently offensive obscenity), goes back to the reason why obscenity is not given any First Amendment protection at all — because it is "patently offensive." On the other hand, if the state prohibits only obscene depictions of Republicans (or Democrats), strict scrutiny would apply because political affiliation has nothing to do with the reasons why obscenity is unprotected. In *Virginia v. Black*, 538 U.S. 343 (2003), the Supreme Court applied the special virulence exception to a statute that singled out cross burning as a prohibited form of intimidation, though it ultimately voided the statute on other grounds.

Finally, laws that target bias-motivated speech are treated differently under the First Amendment than laws that address bias-motivated conduct. Compare the ordinance the Court struck down in *R.A.V.*, with the statute it upheld in *Wisconsin v. Mitchell*, 508 U.S. 476 (1993). *Mitchell* involved a sentence enhancement provision that increased the penalty for racially motivated crimes. The Court rejected the defendant's First Amendment challenge, and distinguished *R.A.V.*, holding that the legislature's "desire to redress the greater individual and societal harm inflicted by bias-inspired conduct provided an adequate explanation for the provision over and above mere disagreement with the offenders' beliefs or biases." *Id.* at 488.

Practice Tip: Students often find it difficult to distinguish between speech in the form of "fighting words" and speech that constitutes a "true threat." A "true threat" conveys an intent to commit an act of unlawful violence, even if the speaker did not actually intend to carry out the threat. *See Virginia v. Black*, 538 U.S. 343 (2003). Thus, while the fighting words doctrine aims to avoid a violent altercation, the true threats doctrine discourages speech that would place another person in fear, separate and apart from whether the threat would also provoke a fight. Note also that a police officer confronted with a "true threat" will not be held to the same level of heightened restraint expected in a "fighting words" case.

Furthermore, as mentioned previously, don't forget to review the wording and history of the applicable statute to determine whether it is unconstitutionally vague or overbroad. You may need to research whether the statute has been authoritatively construed by a state court, and always be sure that the jury instructions are constitutionally firm. Refer to Chapter 14 for more on the vagueness and overbreadth doctrines.

EXERCISE 3

You are an assistant district attorney assigned to handle the case against Martha Jones, an anti-war activist who was arrested at the airport on August 19, while wearing a shirt with the words "Real Patriots Don't Kill Iraqi Children." At the time of the arrest, Jones was standing next to a designated "welcome area" where returning soldiers would reunite with their family. A security guard instructed her to change the shirt, cover it up, or leave the area immediately. When Jones refused, the guard moved to escort her out of the area. Jones pulled away from the guard, and told him to "fuck off." Before she left the area, she turned back to the guard and screamed "I may as well just come back to blow your head off for supporting this fascist war."

You must determine whether the facts are sufficient to prosecute Ms. Jones, and whether the First Amendment operates as a bar to prosecution.

Required Tasks:

Task 1: Identify facts that will help you determine whether to prosecute Ms. Jones.

Task 2: Assuming the facts are sufficient to support a prosecution, draft a criminal complaint against Ms. Jones that charges her with breaching the peace (the LexisNexis web course contains a form for the complaint that has been started for you).

Practice Skills Utilized:

Skill 1: Factual development

Skill 2: Critical analysis

Skill 3: Criminal pleading

Estimated Time for Completion: Approximately 1 ¼ hours

Level of Difficulty (1 to 5):

**DO NOT PROCEED TO THE NEXT PAGE UNTIL YOU
HAVE COMPLETED THE EXERCISE**

SELF-ASSESSMENT

Required Tasks:

Task 1: Identify facts that will help you determine whether to prosecute Ms. Jones.

Task 2: Assuming the facts are sufficient to support a prosecution, draft a criminal complaint against Ms. Jones that charges her with breaching the peace.

Practice Skills Utilized:

Skill 1: Factual development

Skill 2: Critical analysis

Skill 3: Criminal pleading

Task 1: **Identify facts that will help you determine whether to prosecute Ms. Jones.**

Factual Development: The following questions will help you determine whether Ms. Jones engaged in actual fighting words:

- Why was she at the airport at that date and time: for official business, personal reasons, or to cross paths with the soldiers and their families?

  Was she alone?

- How close was she to the designated "welcome area"?

  Did she have reason to pass the area specifically?

  Was anyone inside the area when she was present?

  If so, were they soldiers in uniform, family members, dignitaries, the press?

- When and how did she get the shirt?

  Had she worn the shirt on a previous occasion?

  What was her reason for wearing it that day, and previously?

  Has anyone reacted to the shirt on a previous occasion?

  Does she know of anyone else with a similar shirt?

Does she know of any reaction they've received from wearing the shirt?

- Did anyone comment to Ms. Jones or the security guard about the shirt?

Did it appear that people were talking amongst themselves about the shirt?

If so, who was it, where were they, and what was said?

- How many security guards were on site?

How many witnessed the confrontation or participated in any way?

Other than her remarks to the security guard, did Ms. Jones do or say anything prior to being asked to leave - did she flail her arms or gesture in any way to the security guard, soldiers in the welcome area, or anyone else in the airport?

- What kind of skills or training do members of the armed services receive, if any, on how to deal with anti-war activists, or with a civilian confrontation generally?

Task 2:	**Assuming the facts are sufficient to support a prosecution, draft a criminal complaint against Ms. Jones that charges her with breaching the peace.**
Criminal Pleading:	Refer to Skills & Values Exercise 3, LexisNexis Web Course: Criminal Complaint
Critical Analysis:	At least three issues are immediately apparent from the fact pattern:

(1) Whether Ms. Jones breached the peace with the words printed on her shirt, the comments she made to the security guard, or both? Can you develop a theory of the case that supports more than one charge against her?

(2) Whether a soldier, like a police officer, is expected to exercise a heightened degree of restraint when confronted with true fighting words? Would a reasonable person expect a soldier to respond to the t-shirt with restraint and composure, or is a violent response especially likely under the circumstances? How is a security guard expected to react under these circumstances?

(3) Whether a designated airport "welcome area" established to reunite returning soldiers with members of their family creates a "captive audience" that is incapable of avoiding intrusive and insulting speech? Is the welcome area analogous to an open courtroom in *Cohen*, or more like the "quiet area" in a public park that leaves visitors unable to avoid obtrusive speech? *See Ward v. Rock Against Racism*, 491 U.S. 781 (1989). Is it practical to expect soldiers and their loved ones to celebrate a homecoming without visiting the welcome area? *Cf. McQueary v. Stumbo*, 453 F. Supp. 2d 975 (E.D. Ky. 2006) (applying "captive audience" rationale to buffer zone drawn to protect funeral attendees from disruptive protests). Alternatively, is it realistic to expect other airport patrons to avoid such areas?

Chapter 4
COMMERCIAL SPEECH

INTRODUCTION

The regulation of commercial speech occurs whenever the government creates standards governing the solicitation or advertisement of the products or services of business enterprises. This type of regulation can take many forms. Commercial speech regulations may specify where or when an advertisement or solicitation may occur, how the advertisement or solicitation may be made, or what information may be transmitted in the advertisement or solicitation. Sometimes the government regulations even absolutely ban solicitations or advertisements regarding particular products or services.

Commercial speech cases typically arise when a commercial or business enterprise desires to solicit or advertise in a manner prohibited by the applicable regulations. If the enterprise violates the regulations, the promulgating governmental agency will attempt to enforce sanctions against the enterprise for its conduct, and the entity will assert the First Amendment as a defense. In other cases, the enterprise files suit seeking a declaratory judgment that the regulations are invalid under the First Amendment rather than risking penalties for violating the regulations.

Commercial speech issues also arise when an administrative agency reviews advertisements and solicitations before or concurrently with their dissemination to the public. For instance, many state bar organizations regulate attorney advertisements or solicitations, and frequently require the attorney to submit any such advertisements or solicitations to the bar either before or concurrently with their publication to clients.

The Supreme Court adopted a four-part test for analyzing the constitutionality of regulations on commercial speech in *Central Hudson Gas & Electric Corp. v. Public Service Commission*, 447 U.S. 557, 566 (1980). First, in order to be protected under the First Amendment, the expression must concern lawful activity and not be misleading. The government then must assert a substantial governmental interest to regulate the protected commercial speech. The third part analyzes whether the regulation directly advances the governmental interest asserted, and the final part of the *Central Hudson* test requires that the regulation is not more extensive than necessary to serve that interest. Although several Supreme Court Justices have indicated their dissatisfaction with the *Central Hudson* test, and the "not more extensive than necessary" prong has generated some doctrinal inconsistencies, it remains the applicable standard.

Lawyers are especially concerned with one aspect of commercial speech—restrictions on attorney advertising. In *Bates v. State Bar of*

Arizona, 433 U.S. 350, 383-84 (1977), the Supreme Court held that attorney advertising is protected under the First Amendment. Nevertheless, the Court has upheld regulations that prohibit in-person solicitation by an attorney interested in pecuniary gain, *see Ohralik v. Ohio State Bar Association*, 436 U.S. 447, 459-62 (1978), that prohibit written solicitations of a client within thirty days of an accident, *see Florida Bar v. Went For It, Inc.*, 515 U.S. 618, 620-25 (1995), or that are false or misleading in any respect. Yet free speech issues concerning attorney advertising continue to arise.

EXERCISE 4:

You are a member of the Odin State Bar's Advertising Review Committee. Under Odin's State Bar Rules, the Advertising Review Committee is to review, either before or concurrently with a communication's dissemination, "all written, audio, audio-visual, or digital communication published or transmitted to one or more prospective clients for the purpose of obtaining or that actually results in professional representation." As a member of the committee, you must first view any material brought to your attention and determine whether it is subject to review by your committee and whether it violates the applicable state bar rules. If it violates state bar rules, you then must determine whether the advertisement is nonetheless protected under the First Amendment, employing the *Central Hudson* standard. If you conclude that the rule is constitutional and has been violated, you then must report the matter to the appropriate grievance committee.

Prepare a Memorandum for Each Set of Materials to:

Task 1: Analyze whether the material is subject to committee review.

Task 2: Analyze whether the material violates the applicable rules of the State Bar of Odin.

Task 3: Analyze whether the advertisement may be regulated consistent with the First Amendment.

Task 4: Identify additional information that you would want to obtain to assist in your analyses.

Practice Skills Utilized:

Skill 1: Interpretation of ethical rules and regulations

Skill 2: Critical statutory and constitutional analysis

Skill 3: Strategic thinking

Estimated Time for Completion: Approximately 1 hour per set of materials.

Level of Difficulty (1 to 5):

Pertinent Regulation of the State Bar of Odin:

Rule 13.01 Communications Concerning an Attorney's Services

(A) A lawyer shall not make or sponsor a false or misleading communication about the qualifications or the services of any lawyer or firm. A communication is false or misleading if it:

(1) contains a material misrepresentation of fact or law, or omits a fact necessary to make the statement considered as a whole not materially misleading;

(2) contains any reference in a public media advertisement to past successes or results obtained unless

 (i) the lawyer served as lead counsel or was primarily responsible for the result,

 (ii) the amount involved was actually received by client,

 (iii) the reference is accompanied by adequate information regarding the nature of the case or matter and the damages or injuries received by the client, and

 (iv) if the gross amount received is stated, the attorney's fees and litigation expenses withheld from the amount are stated as well;

(3) is likely to create an unjustified expectation about results the lawyer can achieve;

(4) compares the lawyer's services with other lawyers' services, unless the comparison can be substantiated by reference to verifiable, objective data;

(5) designates one or more specific areas of practice in an advertisement or solicitation unless the lawyer is competent to handle legal matters in such an area of practice;

(6) uses an actor or model to portray a client of the lawyer or law firm;

(7) portrays the lawyer with characteristics unrelated to legal competence;

(8) uses a nickname, moniker, motto, or trade name that implies an ability to obtain results; or

(9) depicts a courthouse or a courtroom to indicate the lawyer's legal prowess.

(B) A lawyer shall not accept or continue employment in a matter when that employment was procured by conduct prohibited by this rule. The failure of an attorney to abide by this rule is subject to appropriate discipline.

The following four sets of materials have been brought to the Committee's attention for analysis:

#1—Transcript of Radio Advertisement

When you need a lawyer, there's only one choice — Max "The Pit Bull" Jones. I'm the toughest lawyer in town [dogs growling in the background]. I can obtain money for you even when other lawyers cannot. Listen to what my clients have to say about me:

Voice #1: I went to three other lawyers before I went to see the Pit Bull, but they were all wimps. Max Jones scared the other side into settling my car accident claim for $150,000. Thanks Max "The Pit Bull" Jones!

Voice #2: If you want to get money, there's only one lawyer to see — the Pit Bull. He's tough, he's mean, and he's scary as hell to the other side. I got $300,000 for my claim, even though my sober friends told me the accident was my fault. Thanks Max "The Pit Bull" Jones!

I could go on and on with similar stories. I've gotten those idiotic insurance companies to pay over $100 million to me and my clients. [Dogs start growling in the background again]. So when you need a lawyer, don't forget who to call — Max "The Pit Bull" Jones — 1-800-PIT-BULL. That number again is 1-800-PIT-BULL. [Growling fades out].

#2—Transcript of Radio Interview

NEWS ANCHOR: We have breaking news from the local county courthouse. Over a year ago, a deadly explosion at the XYZ Manufacturing Plant killed 50 workers and injured hundreds of other workers and local residents. The jury in one of the many lawsuits that was filed as a result has just reached a verdict, awarding $10 million to the family of one of the workers, Zip Tucker, who was killed in the explosion. Joining me live for a discussion about this jury verdict is Wright Justice, a local personal injury attorney who is representing a number of the other victims of this tragedy. Mr. Justice, why is this verdict significant?

MR. JUSTICE: Primarily because the jury rejected XYZ's defense that the explosion was merely an unavoidable accident for which it should not be held responsible. Instead, the jury, relying on the company's long history of safety violations, concluded that not only was the company responsible for the damages caused to Mr. Tucker, but that it also had to pay punitive or exemplary damages because its conduct was so outrageous that punishment was warranted.

NEWS ANCHOR: But isn't the amount of the damages awarded here equally outrageous? Is this a case of a jury run amok?

MR. JUSTICE: Actually, I think the jury award was, if anything, too low. In my past experiences handling death cases arising from similar types of plant catastrophes, I've usually been able to obtain higher jury awards, especially in cases where the jury awards punitive damages. The jury mostly awarded the Tucker family economic damages for his future loss income, and awarded relatively modest punitive damages and mental anguish damages. I think a stronger case could have been easily made that more punitive and mental anguish damages should have been awarded, especially considering the net worth and reprehensible conduct of XYZ. I'm certainly going to seek higher damage awards in my cases.

NEWS ANCHOR: Well, that brings up a good point. How will this jury award impact other pending claims against XYZ?

MR. JUSTICE: I'm hopeful that this will induce XYZ to start trying to negotiate a reasonable settlement. And what I think a reasonable settlement will be in my cases is certainly going to be influenced by the $10 million jury award in Mr. Tucker's case and my belief that I could have even obtained a higher jury award.

NEWS ANCHOR: Anything else of significance from today's events?

MR. JUSTICE: It does illustrate the need to obtain competent legal representation in these cases. If you're a victim of this explosion who hasn't yet visited with a lawyer about your claim, please do so soon—the statute of limitations for your claims will soon expire, so you need to get a lawyer now. It's best to get a law firm with experience in these types of claims.

NEWS ANCHOR: Thanks for joining us today, Mr. Justice.

MR. JUSTICE: It was my pleasure.

NEWS ANCHOR: That was Wright Justice, with the local law firm of Justice & Justice. Now in other news stories today . . . .

#3—See LexisNexis Web Course for Materials

#4—See LexisNexis Web Course for Materials

DO NOT PROCEED TO THE NEXT PAGE UNTIL YOU HAVE COMPLETED THE EXERCISE

SELF-ASSESSMENT

Prepare a Memorandum for Each Set of Materials to:

Task 1: Analyzye whether the material is subject to committee review.

Task 2: Analyze whether the material violates the applicable rules of the State Bar of Odin.

Task 3: Analyze whether the advertisement may be regulated consistent with the First Amendment.

Task 4: Identify additional information that you would want to obtain to assist in your analyses.

Practice Skills Utilized:

Skill 1: Interpretation of ethical rules and regulations

Skill 2: Critical statutory and constitutional analysis

Skill 3: Strategic thinking

Task 1: **Analyze whether the material is subject to committee review.**

Regulatory Scope: The Advertising Review Committee is charged with reviewing "all written, audio, audio-visual, or digital communication published or transmitted to one or more prospective clients for the purpose of obtaining or that actually results in professional representation."

Reasoning: The first, third, and fourth sets of materials were clearly published or transmitted to obtain clients for professional representation. But there is some question regarding the authority of the Committee over the second set of materials. Was the radio interview "for the purpose of obtaining ... professional representation"? Did it actually result in some professional representation? Or was it instead intended as informative commentary on an issue of public concern?

The reality is that attorneys frequently hope that providing such public commentary will lead to the acquisition of new clients. Does this mean that such commentary should be subject to the Committee's jurisdiction under the applicable regulations? Or should the Committee's mission be interpreted narrowly to ensure that the First Amendment is not violated by content-based regulations on such speech addressing matters of public concern?

Practice Tip:	You should always ensure that the decisionmaker had the appropriate authority to act. Even if the decisionmaker articulated a defensible rationale, the conclusion will be null and void in the absence of authority to decide the issue.
Task 2:	**Analyze whether the material violates the applicable rules of the State Bar of Odin.**
Rule Analysis:	There are arguments that each set of materials violates at least one of the fictional rules of the State Bar of Odin (please note that this does not indicate that the materials violate the applicable state bar rules of any actual state—this fictional set of rules was compiled from a number of states and then modified in many respects for this problem).
	The first set of materials, regarding Max "The Pit Bull" Jones, has several clear violations of Rule 13.01, and may violate other regulations as well, depending on further factual development (see analysis for Task 4).
	Assuming the second set of materials, the radio interview of Wright Justice, is subject to review by the Advertising Review Committee (see analysis for Task 1), it's a close question whether Rule 13.01 was violated. Did Wright Justice refer to results obtained in his prior cases by stating that he had received higher awards for his clients? Or is this acceptable because this wasn't a "public media advertisement"? Did he create an unjustified expectation that he could obtain better results and did he make unsubstantiated comparisons to other attorneys?
	The third set of materials, the Insurance Adjusters commercial, may run afoul of several sections of fictional Rule 13.01. The commercial contains generic comparisons to other attorneys by claiming "legal lightweights" make "lots of quick settlements" and settle "for ten cents on the dollar." It seems to imply that the firm has a history of past successes, by the adjusters stating they are "no match for them" and this will "cost us a lot of money—again," without providing any information regarding these prior cases. And it arguably creates some expectations regarding the results that will be obtained. But are these references enough to violate Rule 13.01?

The fourth set of materials, the Peter & Paul Law Firm video file, presents other issues under this fictional rule. Does the use of "Christian Trial Lawyers" portray the firm with characteristics unrelated to legal competence? If employing Christian values is related to legal competence, does that mean that the moniker implies an ability to obtain results? Is the use of the courtroom in the background designed to indicate the law firm's prowess? Is using "Christian Trial Lawyers" an implicit comparison to other lawyers that are not Christians?

Task 3: **Analyze whether the advertisement may be regulated consistent with the First Amendment.**

Case Analysis: Although the Supreme Court has held that attorney advertising is protected by the First Amendment, the Court has recognized several substantial governmental interests that may justify its restriction. In addition to the government's overarching interest in precluding misleading advertising and solicitations, the Court has noted substantial governmental interests in protecting consumers, maintaining standards among licensed professions, preserving the privacy of potential clients, and preventing invasive conduct by attorneys. *See, e.g., Ohralik v. Ohio State Bar Association*, 436 U.S. 447, 460-62 (1978). The Court has also indicated that regulations on lawyer advertising may be justified to prevent an "erosion of confidence in the profession," at least when evidentiary support exists that the public perception of attorneys is in decline as a result of the advertising. *Florida Bar v. Went for It, Inc.*, 515 U.S. 618, 635 (1995).

Reasoning: The first set of materials, concerning Max "The Pit Bull Jones," may be misleading and therefore not entitled to First Amendment protection. Is it misleading to use the name "The Pit Bull"? Does this depend on whether Max Jones is generally known by friends and family as "Pit Bull," or whether this was merely a marketing ploy? Are the unsubstantiated comparisons to other attorneys and the results obtained without the necessary disclosures misleading to the average consumer? What about his portrayal as "mean and scary"? If such statements are misleading, no constitutional protection exists, and the matter should be referred to the grievance committee. If the statements are not misleading, then does the prohibition of these statements directly advance a substantial governmental interest without being more extensive than necessary to serve that interest? Is there a substantial governmental interest in maintaining the dignity of the legal profession? Are the regulations more extensive than necessary to advance this interest? Could the regulations be upheld on the basis that they protect the privacy of potential clients or prevent invasive conduct by attorneys?

With respect to the second set of materials, the radio interview of Wright Justice, the initial issue is whether this is commercial speech at all. The Supreme Court has not provided a very precise distinction between commercial and non-commercial speech, with the Court essentially implying that the distinction is a matter of common sense. *See, e.g., Ohralik*, 436 U.S. at 455-56. The Court has described "commercial speech" as "expression related solely to the economic interests of the speaker and its audience" and as "'speech proposing a commercial transaction, which occurs in an area traditionally subject to governmental regulation.'" *Central Hudson Gas & Electric Corp. v. Public Service Commission*, 447 U.S. 557, 561-62 (1980) (quoting *Ohralik*, 436 U.S. at 455-56). Was the radio interview solely related to the economic interests of the speaker and the audience? Did it propose a commercial transaction? As a matter of common sense, was the interview "commercial speech" or some other variety of speech?

If the interview is not "commercial speech," the constitutionality of applying Odin's State Bar Rules to the interview will be governed by other First Amendment doctrines. If the interview is considered commercial speech, there would still be the question whether the State Bar regulations are more extensive than necessary to directly advance a substantial governmental interest. The strongest governmental interest would be protecting consumers from misleading information, but would applying these regulations to all attorney communications, even those commenting on a matter of public concern, be a reasonable fit for serving this interest?

The constitutional question with respect to the third set of materials, the Insurance Adjusters commercial, again depends on whether the advertisement is misleading and whether applying Rule 13.01 in this context is more extensive than necessary to directly advance a substantial governmental interest. Do the commercial's broad brushed criticisms of "legal lightweights" that settle quick and cheaply mislead anyone? And considering that the insurance company portrayed in the commercial, named the Strong Armed Insurance Company, is clearly fictional, would the average consumer be misled by the claims that the firm has cost this fictional insurance company lots of money? Would the average consumer understand that this is a parody? If the commercial is not misleading, what other governmental interest would be sufficient to regulate it? Is it just a matter that the parody in the advertisement, at least in the minds of some, may be demeaning to the legal profession? Is that enough of a governmental interest, without evidentiary support of the public's perceptions, for regulation?

The fourth set of materials, the Peter & Paul Law Firm video file, is neither false nor misleading, as the basis and meaning of the moniker is explained. Thus, the issue is whether the regulations, if interpreted to prevent the use of the term "Christian Trial Lawyers" and the depiction of courtrooms, is more extensive than necessary to directly advance a substantial governmental interest. What substantial governmental interest is at stake in regulating these advertisements? Is preventing the firm from using "Christian Trial Lawyers" more extensive than necessary to directly advance any such substantial governmental interest? Is preventing the firm from using depictions of the courtroom more extensive than necessary to directly advance any such substantial governmental interest?

Task 4: **Identify additional information that you would want to obtain to assist in your analyses.**

Strategic Thinking: What other information would have been helpful? Did you think about in the first set of materials whether the "voices" of the clients were the actual clients or were actors? Was Max Jones known as "The Pit Bull" even before he started practicing law? Is it possible that Max Jones isn't competent to handle these types of cases? Should you investigate the experience of the other attorneys to ensure that they have a sufficient level of expertise? And should you investigate whether any of the other statements are false and misleading? Would it help to attempt to conduct studies regarding how certain advertisements impact public perceptions of the legal profession?

Chapter 5
Time, Place and Manner Restrictions

Introduction

Much of what that takes place in law school might be described as "passive learning." Your primary task as a law student is to discern the rule of law as announced in appellate cases and understand the reasoning that leads to a particular outcome. Surely this is no small task, particularly when First Amendment cases are concerned, but it differs markedly from tasks that require active reasoning.

Active reasoning requires that you assess the validity of the information you are given based on prior knowledge. For example, passive learning was involved when you read *Clark v. Community for Creative Non-Violence*, 468 U.S. 288 (1984) and *Ward v. Rock Against Racism*, 491 U.S. 781 (1989), to discern the applicable test in a time, place or manner case. Conversely, active reasoning occurs when you apply that test to a particular fact pattern. It also occurs when you are asked on an exam whether a hypothetical court applied the appropriate rule of law under the circumstances. Rather than accept the validity of the court's judgment, you critically analyze whether the judgment is consistent with established constitutional standards.

As a lawyer, you will continue to engage in passive learning whenever you research the applicable law that applies to your client's case. Other tasks require a higher level of engagement. Opinion drafting and appellate advocacy are two such examples.

If you work as a judicial clerk following law school, you will be asked to review draft opinions, and may even be asked to compose the first draft of an opinion that ultimately will be published under your judge's name. In doing so, your job is to minimize the risk that your judge's opinion will be overturned on appeal. You must therefore learn to spot errors or misstatements of law in written material before they are incorporated into a final opinion.

The same critical inquiry is required when a practicing lawyer seeks to appeal an adverse judgment. Effective appellate advocacy requires not only that you understand the basis for the trial court's conclusion, but that you identify points of law the trial court misapplied. The cases in your text book reached the appellate level precisely because a skillful lawyer identified fatal errors in the lower court's judgment.

Think of the following time, place and manner problem as an exercise in active reasoning. It requires that you understand the relevant constitutional doctrine and that you affirmatively engage that knowledge to determine whether and how a draft judicial opinion should be revised.

A content-neutral time, place or manner regulation is constitutional if it is narrowly tailored to serve a substantial government interest that is unrelated to expression, and leaves open ample alternative channels for communication. Remember that here, the narrow tailoring inquiry is significantly less demanding than it is under a content-based strict scrutiny case. Also, be sure you understand the difference between a time, place and manner analysis under *Clark* and *Ward*, and an analysis of speech related conduct under *United States v. O'Brien*, 391 U.S. 367 (1968), particularly as it relates to regulations on the "manner" of speech.

TIME, PLACE AND MANNER RESTRICTIONS 53

Exercise 5

You are a law clerk working for a judge who has asked you to review a draft opinion she wrote in a case involving a First Amendment challenge to a security perimeter that surrounds the San Francisco Convention Center. Your job is to identify any problems with the opinion that might provide a basis for appeal.

Required Tasks:

Task 1: Identify erroneous statements of law or unclear passages in the draft opinion.

Task 2: Revise the opinion to correct any misstatements of law, and include appropriate citations to cases (the LexisNexis Web Course contains a version of the opinion that you can revise).

Practice Skills Utilized:

Skill 1: Legal analysis

Skill 2: Opinion drafting

Estimated Time for Completion: Approximately 45 minutes

Level of Difficulty (1 to 5):

DRAFT OPINION-NOT APPROVED FOR PUBLICATION

City of San Francisco v. American Free Speech Union, et al. United States District Court, Northern District of California

ROBERTA J. KROGER, District Judge.

This case involves a First Amendment challenge to a security perimeter surrounding a new Convention Center in San Francisco, California. The controversy arises from the following facts.

I. Facts

The San Francisco Convention Center is scheduled to open in three weeks with its first official event, the annual California Chili Cook-off. Over the next 12 months, a number of conventions, meetings, concerts, political rallies and entertainment events are scheduled to take place at the Convention Center.

The Convention Center grounds include several large parking lots adjacent to four small buildings, and a large, circular enclosed building used as the main exhibit hall. The hall has a capacity to hold up to 20,000 people, and another five to eight thousand people can assemble on the grounds outside.

Cage Free is a non-profit group that seeks to draw public attention to major food production companies that fail to comply with federal regulations regarding the ethical treatment of animals. The group plans to hold a rally at the Chili Cook-off to protest several such companies whose products will be featured there. Cage Free asserts that a security perimeter established on the grounds of the Convention Center unconstitutionally interferes with its right of free speech by restricting access to a public forum.

Following a review of security measures undertaken in Boston, Chicago and New York, the San Francisco City Council voted to establish a designated security perimeter at all Convention Center events. The relevant municipal code states that the perimeter is meant "to provide security at Convention Center events by deterring attacks involving explosives and weapons."

The security perimeter includes a "Public Demonstration Zone" where Cage Free can assemble for purposes of holding a rally or engaging in public protest. The Zone is located on a sidewalk 200 feet from one of four entrances to the Center. Though individuals who seek to access the Convention Center must pass through a security screening, no such screening is required of persons inside the Zone. The Zone is enclosed by two rings of concrete barriers set eight feet apart that aid in the apprehension of protestors who evade the inner barrier. No obstructions blocks the area between the sidewalk and the edge of the Zone, so anyone wishing to do so could walk to the outer concrete barrier and be within eight feet of the demonstrators inside.

II. Analysis

Neither Congress nor the states may make a law "abridging the freedom of speech... or the right of the people peaceably to assemble...." But First Amendment rights are not absolute, and the government may impose reasonable restrictions on the time, place, and manner of speech in a public forum. This type of restriction is constitutional as long as: (1) it is justified without regard to the content of the speech; (2) it is narrowly tailored to serve a significant government interest; and (3) ample alternative channels for communication of the desired message remain available. Where a First Amendment violation is alleged, the complaining party must prove that the restrictions affect protected expression in a traditional public forum and do not meet the three elements of the time, place, and manner test.

Time, place or manner restrictions must be narrowly tailored to serve a significant governmental interest. The court finds that preventing the likelihood of a security breach at the San Francisco Convention Center warrants some kind of government action, and therefore proceeds to the narrow tailoring analysis.

A government restriction on speech is narrowly tailored if there are "no alternative means that would more precisely and narrowly" meet the government's objective. *U.S. v. O'Brien*, 391 U.S. 367, 381 (1968). In other words, if the regulation burdens more speech than necessary to further the significant governmental interest, it impermissibly infringes upon First Amendment rights.

Moreover, broad, generic recitals of "security concerns" may not be used to automatically validate burdens on First Amendment rights. Rather, the government must demonstrate that particular measures are needed to protect against foreseeable harms caused by the party denied access a public forum. *Ward v. Rock Against Racism*, 491 U.S. 781, 801 (1989). The regulation's effectiveness is not judged by considering all the hypothetical groups that might some day use the facility. *Clark v. Community for Creative Non-Violence*, 468 U.S. 288, 296–97 (1984).

To justify the security plan, the City points specifically to concerns about attacks by weapons and explosive devices. While these are indeed grave concerns, the security plan affects more speech than necessary to further these interests. Under the proposed security plan, individuals who wish to enter the Zone are not subject to security screening; only individuals who enter the Convention Center are screened. The City could require all demonstrators or protestors to undergo a rigorous security screening before entering the Zone; thereby allowing an opportunity to temporarily confiscate non-speech-related items. The Zone could then be moved closer to the Convention Center and to the participants' path.

Moreover, as situated, the Zone significantly interferes with Cage Free's ability to reach its intended audience. While individuals who enter through the main entry gate come within view and earshot of protesters stationed in the Zone, alternative points of entry are far from the designated protest vicinity. The resulting burden on Cage Free's ability to reach a desired audience works a direct and substantial harm to their First Amendment interests in a way that has not been tolerated in similar cases. See *Ward v. Rock Against Racism*, 491 U.S. 781, 802–03 (1989).

III. Conclusion

The security plan is not narrowly tailored to advance the important governmental interests at play in this case. The restricted protest Zone burdens more speech than is necessary in a manner that fails the second prong of the time, place, and manner standard of review. As such, a permanent injunction is granted against the City and the security plan must be revised so as not to impermissibly infringe upon fundamental First Amendment rights.

DO NOT PROCEED TO THE NEXT PAGE UNTIL YOU HAVE COMPLETED THE EXERCISE

SELF-ASSESSMENT

Required Tasks:

Task 1: Identify erroneous statements of law or unclear passages in the draft opinion.

Task 2: Revise the opinion to correct any misstatements of law, and include appropriate citations to cases.

Practice Skills Utilized:

Skill 1: Legal analysis

Skill 2: Opinion drafting

Task 1: **Identify erroneous statements of law or unclear passages in the draft opinion.**

Legal Analysis:

1. "The complaining party must prove that the restrictions do not meet the time, place or manner test."

2. "Time, place or manner restrictions must be narrowly tailored to serve a significant governmental interest."

3. "The court finds that preventing the likelihood of a security breach at the San Francisco Convention Center warrants some kind of government action ..."

4. "A government restriction on speech is narrowly tailored if there are 'no alternative means that would more precisely and narrowly' meet the government's objective. *U.S. v. O'Brien*, 391 U.S. 367, 381 (1968). If the regulation burdens more speech than necessary to further the significant governmental interest, it impermissibly infringes upon First Amendment rights."

5. "Though individuals who access the Convention Center through the main entrance follow a path that is within view and earshot of protesters stationed in the Zone, alternative points of entry are nonetheless available through which individuals can access the Center without passing protesters. The resulting burden on Cage Free's ability to reach a desired audience works a direct and substantial harm to their First Amendment interests

in a way that a permissible restriction would not. See *Ward v. Rock Against Racism*, 491 U.S. 781, 802–03 (1989)."

6. "[T]he government must demonstrate that particular measures are needed to protect against foreseeable harms caused by the party denied access a public forum. *Ward v. Rock Against Racism*, 491 U.S. 781, 801 (1989). The regulation's effectiveness is not judged by considering all the hypothetical groups that might some day use the facility. *Clark v. Community for Creative Non-Violence*, 468 U.S. 288, 296–97 (1984)."

7. Did the court address all of the required elements under a TPM analysis?

Task 2:

Revise the opinion to correct any misstatements of law, and include appropriate citations to cases.

Opinion Drafting

1. "The complaining party must prove that the restrictions do not meet the time, place or manner test."

    Consider: Did you correct this statement to correctly identify which party has the burden in a TPM case?

2. "Time, place or manner restrictions must be narrowly tailored to serve a significant governmental interest."

    Consider: This statement is only partly true. Did you revise the statement for accuracy?

3. "The court finds that preventing the likelihood of a security breach at the San Francisco Convention Center warrants some kind of government action ..."

    Consider: Whether this finding is sufficient under the circumstances is at least debatable. Did you consider *City of Renton v. Playtime Theaters, Inc.*, 475 U.S. 41, 51–52 (1986), and whether secondary effects cases are sufficiently distinguishable such that San

Francisco should be required to conduct its own studies before erecting a security perimeter?

4. "A government restriction on speech is narrowly tailored if there are 'no alternative means that would more precisely and narrowly' meet the government's objective. *U.S. v. O'Brien*, 391 U.S. 367, 381 (1968). If the regulation burdens more speech than necessary to further the significant governmental interest, it impermissibly infringes upon First Amendment rights."

   Consider: Though *O'Brien* is a symbolic conduct case, the Supreme Court later said that its analysis differed little, if at all, from the standard that applied to TPM restrictions. *Clark v. Community For Creative Non-Violence*, 468 U.S. 288, 298 n.8 (1984). Does the quoted language accurately reflect the standard that applies to a true time, place or manner test? What makes this a time, place or manner case under *Clark* and *Ward*, and not a symbolic conduct case under *O'Brien*?

5. "Though individuals who access the Convention Center through the main entrance follow a path that is within view and earshot of protesters stationed in the Zone, alternative points of entry are nonetheless available through which individuals can access the Center without passing protesters. The resulting burden on Cage Free's ability to reach a desired audience works a direct and substantial harm to their First Amendment interests in a way that a permissible restriction would not. See *Ward v. Rock Against Racism*, 491 U.S. 781, 802–03 (1989)."

   Consider: Did you consider whether the sound-amplification restrictions in *Ward* provide an adequate analogy, and whether Cage Free has more or less access to a desired audience?

6. "[T]he government must demonstrate that particular measures are needed to protect against foreseeable harms caused by the party denied access a public forum. See *Ward v. Rock Against Racism*, 491 U.S. 781, 801 (1989). The regulation's effectiveness is not judged by considering all the hypothetical groups that might some day use the facility. *Clark v. Community for Creative Non-Violence*, 468 U.S. 288, 296–97 (1984)."

   Consider: Did you identify this as an erroneous statement of law? Did your revision account for the relevance of future events and a larger venue capacity?

7. Did the court address all of the required elements of a TPM analysis?

   Consider: Did you identify which element the court overlooked? Is the additional analysis required in this case?

Chapter 6
PUBLIC EMPLOYEE SPEECH RIGHTS

INTRODUCTION

Public employee speech cases arise in an "enormous variety of fact situations" in which a governmental employer fires or disciplines an employee because of his or her expression. *Pickering v. Board of Education*, 391 U.S. 563, 569 (1968). The Supreme Court's decisions have considered such varied circumstances as writing a letter to the editor of the local paper, providing an internal school memorandum to a local radio station for public broadcast, complaining of racial discrimination privately to a superior at work, preparing and distributing an unauthorized internal office questionnaire regarding employee morale, expressing privately to a co-worker a desire for a successful presidential assassination, accepting honoraria for articles and speaking engagements, and moonlighting by selling sexually explicit videotapes on eBay. The expression at issue can thus take place either at work or after working hours, as long as the employer uses the expression as the basis for employment-related discipline.

Public employee speech cases typically reach a private attorney after the public employee has been terminated or disciplined. The attorney must investigate whether the disciplinary action is due to constitutionally protected employee expression. Attorneys for the government then defend any resulting suit, although occasionally the public employer has the foresight to seek legal advice before terminating or disciplining the employee for expressive activities.

The expression of public employees is protected from job retaliation under the First Amendment only if a number of hurdles are satisfied. First, only employees who speak "as a citizen" are protected, which means that there is no constitutional protection from employer discipline for statements made pursuant to an employee's "official duties." *Garcetti v. Ceballos*, 547 U.S. 410, 421 (2006). Second, to be protected, the expression must address a "matter of public concern." *Connick v. Myers*, 461 U.S. 138, 147 (1983). Assuming the first two hurdles are satisfied, the third step balances the state's interest in providing efficient governmental services against the individual and public interests in the speech at issue. *Pickering*, 391 U.S. at 568. The fourth and final inquiry then analyzes as a factual matter whether the speech was the basis for the adverse employment action, providing the government an opportunity to avoid liability if it establishes that it would have undertaken the same action irrespective of the employee's protected speech. *Mount Healthy City School District Board of Education v. Doyle*, 429 U.S. 274, 285–87 (1977).

The Supreme Court's holding in *Garcetti* that speech made pursuant to an employee's job duties is not entitled to any protection from retaliation has caused some confusion in the lower courts. The *Garcetti* Court provided very little guidance on ascertaining the scope of an employee's duties, other than rejecting the premise that employers can confidently rely on "excessively broad descriptions." 547 U.S. at 424–25. The Court explained that listing a particular task in a formal job description, which often does not resemble the employee's actual duties, is "neither necessary nor sufficient" to constitute official duty unprotected speech. Instead, the query is a "practical one." *Id.* But the lower courts have divergent views on how to undertake this "practical" task.

EXERCISE 6:

You are an attorney in private practice who has been approached by John Smith. Mr. Smith had been employed as a bookkeeper in the local county tax collection department. He subsequently reported his belief that a co-worker was swindling the department of a large amount of money. Like other county employees, he is required to "disclose waste, fraud, abuse, and corruption to appropriate authorities." But soon after his report, he is terminated by his employer. He comes to you seeking your advice as to whether he has a claim for wrongful termination.

Required Tasks:

Task 1: Research what must be proven in your jurisdiction for Mr. Smith to recover.

Task 2: Prepare a list of additional information that you need to develop from Mr. Smith concerning his claim before representing him.

Task 3: Assuming that you develop enough information to represent Mr. Smith, draft a set of discovery requests to the government for his case (the LexisNexis Web Course contains forms for the discovery requests that have been started for you).

Practice Skills Utilized:

Skill 1: Legal research
Skill 2: Legal analysis
Skill 3: Strategic thinking
Skill 4: Legal drafting

Estimated Time for Completion: Approximately 2 hours

Level of Difficulty (1 to 5):

Practice Tip: Your discovery requests should in large part mirror the legal elements of the claim identified in your legal research. Some astute attorneys even actually draft an initial proposed jury charge or proposed conclusions of law before engaging in any discovery to ensure that their discovery requests obtain all the necessary information for each element of their client's claims.

DO NOT PROCEED TO THE NEXT PAGE UNTIL YOU HAVE COMPLETED THE EXERCISE

SELF-ASSESSMENT

Required Tasks:

Task 1: Research what must be proven in your jurisdiction for Mr. Smith to recover.

Task 2: Prepare a list of additional information that you need to develop from Mr. Smith concerning his claim before representing him.

Task 3: Assuming that you develop enough information to represent Mr. Smith, draft a set of discovery requests to the government for his case.

Practice Skills Utilized:

Skill 1: Legal research
Skill 2: Legal analysis
Skill 3: Strategic thinking
Skill 4: Legal drafting

Task 1: **Research what must be proven in your jurisdiction for Mr. Smith to recover.**

Legal Research & Analysis: As discussed in the introduction, to recover in a public employee speech retaliation case under the First Amendment, Mr. Smith would need to prove (1) that he made the report "as a citizen," (2) that it addressed a matter of "public concern," (3) that his interest in making the report was not outweighed by the government's interest in providing effective and efficient services through its agencies, and (4) that the report was a substantial factor in his discharge. The most difficult legal issue would be determining the proper approach for analyzing whether the report was "citizen speech" because it was not part of Smith's job duties.

There are three different approaches for analyzing this problem. The first approach interprets *Garcetti* narrowly to apply only to speech that "the employer itself has commissioned or created." 547 U.S. at 421–22. Under this view, only speech that is *required* by the job would be outside the ambit of the First Amendment. If an employee has discretion whether to make the comments or pursue the investigation, the *Garcetti* bar does not apply, and the speech might be protected *Cf. Cioffi v. Averill Park Central School District Board of Education*, 444 F.3d 158, 167 (2d Cir. 2006).

A drawback to this narrow approach is that it may conflict with another concern *Garcetti* articulated — to avoid committing the judiciary to an "intrusive role" overseeing "communications between and among government employees and their superiors in the course of official business." 547 U.S. at 423. Due to this concern, some other courts have adopted a broad approach, finding any employee speech related to the tasks performed on the job unprotected. *Cf. Callahan v. Fermon*, 526 F.3d 1040, 1045 (7th Cir. 2008). Yet this broad approach is in tension with some of the precedents reaffirmed in *Garcetti*, such as *Givhan v. West Line Consolidated School District*, 439 U.S. 410, 414 (1979), which held that a public school teacher's complaints to her principal, based on the school's racial discrimination in hiring teachers, were protected from retaliation.

A compromise position between the narrow and broad approaches analyzes whether disciplining the employee would silence his or her ability to participate in public affairs. This approach finds support in *Garcetti*'s assertion that the "theoretical underpinnings" for public employee speech rights hinges upon an "analogue to speech by citizens who are not government employees." This approach considers whether the employee's speech is similar to non-public employee expression regarding the government. *Cf. Davis v. McKinney*, 518 F.3d 304, 313–17 (5th Cir. 2008); *Freitag v. Ayers*, 468 F.3d 528, 545–46 (9th Cir. 2006).

Because the Supreme Court has not resolved the appropriate approach, you first need to determine whether binding precedent exists in your jurisdiction. In the absence of such binding precedent, you need to be prepared to develop your case under each of the various approaches.

The legal standards regarding the other elements for recovery are less difficult. A matter of public concern includes any "matter of political, social, or other concern to the community." *Connick v. Myers*, 461 U.S. 138, 146–47 (1983). A public employee swindling from the public coffers should meet this standard. The balancing analysis will depend greatly on the legitimacy of Mr. Smith's concerns — if Mr. Smith objectively had strong evidence to support his suspicions, his interest and the public interest in the report probably will outweigh the employer's interest in efficiency. On the other hand, if such objective evidence is lacking, an unsupported accusation against a co-worker is exactly the type of friction that an employer may be authorized to snuff out despite the expressive rights at issue. Finally, Mr. Smith would need to establish that his speech was a substantial factor in his discharge, and be prepared to rebut any claim that the government would have fired him in the absence of his report.

Practice Tip: Another avenue to explore, outside First Amendment doctrine, is state whistleblowing statutes or state employment causes of action that may provide Mr. Smith greater protection. Do not become so focused on constitutional claims in practice that you miss the existence of a statutory or common law claim that might be more advantageous to your client.

Task 2: Prepare a list of additional information that you need to develop from Mr. Smith concerning his claim before representing him.

Strategic Thinking: Before you agree to represent Mr. Smith, you will need to obtain a great deal more information regarding his report and his job performance to see if a First Amendment or other claim can be asserted consistent with an attorney's ethical obligation to ensure that the legal and factual contentions in a lawsuit are adequately supported. Some potential areas that you would want to address, in order to ensure that you can meet all the elements of a First Amendment retaliation claim, include:

1. A description of his daily duties as a bookkeeper;
2. The basis for his belief that the other employee was swindling the state;
3. His motivation for filing his report;
4. Whether he had ever made such a report previously;
5. Any personal or work-related difficulties with the other employee before his report;
6. Any personal or work-related difficulties with others in his department;

7. Everyone he told about the swindling accusation and their positions;

8. Any warnings or disciplinary actions from his supervisors for poor job performance before his report;

9. The basis for his belief that he was terminated for making the report;

10. Any threats or warnings that he had received not to make the report;

11. The impact his report had on workplace morale and working relationships;

12. His prior salary, and his current employment status and income; and

13. Any evidence of mental anguish or other damages from the termination.

Task 3: **Assuming that you develop enough information to represent Mr. Smith, draft a set of discovery requests to the government for his case.**

Legal Drafting: The interrogatories and requests for production that you developed should attempt to obtain similar information from the government as in your interview of Mr. Smith. You would need to ensure that you properly requested, among other things:

1. A copy of his job duties from the employee manual;

2. His written work product while employed in the department;

3. Information regarding the daily tasks performed by other bookkeepers;

4. Whether similar reports of swindling had been made by any other employee;

5. Mr. Smith's personnel file, including all performance evaluations;

6. Documentation regarding the impact his report had on morale and working relationships;

7. The identity of the person who made the decision to fire him;

8. All documents related to the reasons for his termination;

9. All communications made related to the reasons for his termination;
10. The identity and job description of all persons who viewed his report;
11. The results of any investigation into the swindling accusation; and
12. The personnel file of the allegedly swindling employee.

Be sure to carefully draft your discovery requests seeking this information. You want to ensure that they are broad enough to encompass all relevant and material information, without being so broad as to allow your opponent to properly refuse to respond on grounds of harassment and overbreadth. For example, a request to "produce all documents in any way related to John Smith" would be objectionable, although a request to "produce all documents contained in the personnel file of John Smith, including but not limited to his performance evaluations or reviews, attendance records, promotion history, and written documentation of his termination" would be appropriate.

You also have an ethical responsibility under both Federal Rule of Civil Procedure 26(g) and Model Rule of Professional Conduct 3.4 to refrain from discovery requests that are merely designed to harass, cause unnecessary delay, or needlessly increase the costs of litigation. Thus, you must ensure that your discovery requests are relevant to your claims or the anticipated defenses of your opponent.

Chapter 7
PUBLIC SCHOOL STUDENTS' SPEECH RIGHTS

INTRODUCTION

Public school students do not "shed their constitutional rights to freedom of speech or expression at the schoolhouse gate." *Tinker v. Des Moines Independent School District*, 393 U.S. 503, 506 (1969). Nevertheless, due to the special characteristics and purpose of the school environment, "the constitutional rights of students in public school are not automatically coextensive with the rights of adults in other settings." *Bethel School District No. 403 v. Fraser*, 478 U.S. 675, 682 (1986). As a result, resolving a free speech claim asserted by a public school student requires balancing the expressive rights of the student against the interests of his or her classmates and the government in creating a meaningful and secure educational environment.

Public school speech cases arise when a school adopts or enforces a policy prohibiting specified student expression, or a public school official disciplines or penalizes a student based on the student's expressive activities. Although usually the cases involve expression occurring either at school or during school-sponsored extracurricular activities, some cases have addressed off-campus expression directed at a school teacher or administrator, such as belittling or threatening references to school officials on a website or blog. Whether the offending speech occurs either on or off campus, the attorney for the school district typically learns of the controversy through a school administrator, with the parents or guardians of the student obtaining representation for their child.

In *Tinker*, the Supreme Court announced, as a general rule, that regulation of public school student speech was only appropriate when the speech would "materially and substantially interfere with the requirements of appropriate discipline in the operation of the school." 393 U.S. at 509. But subsequently, the Court has qualified that the *Tinker* standard is not appropriate in every situation. For instance, if the speech is sponsored by the school or can be fairly characterized as part of the school curriculum, educators do not need to demonstrate a material and substantial interference, but only that their actions are "reasonably related to legitimate pedagogical concerns." *Hazelwood School District v. Kuhlmeier*, 484 U.S. 260, 273 (1988). Additionally, public school officials have more leeway to regulate certain topics of student speech, allowing them, for example, to prohibit student speech during school or a school-sponsored event that promotes illegal drug use, *see Morse v. Frederick*, 551 U.S. 393 (2007), or that is sexually explicit or vulgar, *see Fraser*, 478 U.S. at 684–84.

These standards, however, are often difficult to apply. When is a school activity part of the school curriculum? What must be shown for a material and substantial disruption of appropriate discipline? What other topics, if any, should be subject to less stringent scrutiny? Both school administrators and attorneys frequently must grapple with such problems.

EXERCISE 7:

You represent Peter Phillips, a sixth grade public school student at Eagle Elementary School. You have filed a complaint in federal court alleging Peter's free speech rights were violated when he was not allowed to distribute cards he had created to accompany a school project. Defendant Grand Independent School District has just filed a motion for summary judgment, as follows, which you will need to respond to:

UNITED STATES DISTRICT COURT
WESTERN DISTRICT OF OLYMPIA

PETER PHILLIPS, a minor, by and through his parents, PAUL & MONICA PHILLIPS, Plaintiff v. GRAND INDEPENDENT SCHOOL DIST. et al., Defendants	CIVIL ACTION NO. 09-7213

DEFENDANT GRAND INDEPENDENT SCHOOL DISTRICT'S MOTION FOR SUMMARY JUDGMENT AND BRIEF IN SUPPORT

Defendant Grand Independent School District moves for summary judgment under Federal Rule of Civil Procedure 56. Based on the attached evidence, there is no genuine issue of material fact as to the Plaintiff's free speech claim against the District, and it should be dismissed.

I. The Undisputed Facts Entitle the District to Summary Judgment

The following facts are undisputed:

1. As part of the sixth grade curriculum at Eagle Elementary, students participated in an exercise called "Classroom City." The students were required to create, market, and "sell" a homemade product made for under $10. Other students would then "purchase" the products with fake classroom money provided as part of the exercise. The stores would be monitored to determine which students accumulated the most money through the sale of their products. See Skidder Affidavit.

2. The guidelines for the assignment prohibited selling any food products or games of chance. The guidelines also required that a prototype of the product had to submitted before the Classroom City exercise to conduct a marketing survey of a representative sample of the student body to determine how much inventory was needed. Skidder Aff.

3. Peter Phillips submitted a prototype of a cardboard mask designed as a devil or demon for the marketing survey. Jones Dep.

4. Even though no message had been included with Peter's product prototype, Peter's father made him small white cards with black printing to attach on the back of the cardboard masks that Peter "sold" during Classroom City. These cards read as follows:

> These masks are undoubtedly scary. But they are not nearly as scary as the damage done by the darkest of lords, the Vice President, and his minion, the President, to the nation we all love.

5. During Classroom City, Peter "sold" a mask with a card attached to its underside to a fellow student, Charlie Drove. Charlie became upset after he turned the mask over and saw the card attached to the back, especially because his family supported the President. He ran to his teacher, Mrs. Jones, with tears in his eyes. Jones Dep.

6. After examining the mask and attached card Charlie brought her, Mrs. Jones immediately went to discuss the matter with Assistant Principal Skidder, who supervised the Classroom City exercise. After reading the card, Skidder was concerned about the card's political content and whether other students might be offended. Although Skidder offered to allow Peter to "sell" the mask with his cards in the parking lot after school, he refused to allow Peter to continue to "sell" the mask and cards during the Classroom City exercise. Skidder Aff.; Jones Dep.

7. Peter decided to just sell the mask without the cards during the Classroom City exercise rather than attempting to distribute the cards in the parking lot. Peter received an "A" for the Classroom City project, and he was not disciplined for attempting to sell the masks with the political cards. Jones Dep.

II. Peter's Free Speech Rights Were Not Violated Because the School's Actions Were Reasonably Related to Legitimate Concerns

Hazelwood is the appropriate standard to apply to this case. Under *Hazelwood*, a school may regulate speech that is either part of the school's curriculum or is sponsored by the school as long as the regulation is reasonably related to legitimate pedagogical concerns. 484 U.S. 260, 273 (1988). In this case, this standard was undoubtedly satisfied.

It is undisputed that Classroom City was part of the sixth grade curriculum. According to the Supreme Court, *Hazelwood* applies whenever the "activities may fairly be characterized as part of the school curriculum, whether or not they occur in a traditional classroom setting, so long as they are supervised by faculty members and designed to impart particular knowledge or skills to student participants and audiences." *Id.* at 271. Peter's expression was part of a curricular assignment, which did not invite personal views or viewpoints. As a result, the decision to prevent Peter from distributing the card only had to be reasonable.

Here, it was reasonable to prevent the distribution of the card to prevent other students from being offended and upset, as Charlie was. The determination that the political card should not be distributed during Classroom City was the product of a reasonable evaluation of legitimate pedagogical concerns and should not be disturbed by the federal courts.

WHEREFORE, Defendant respectfully requests that this Court grant summary judgment and render a take-nothing judgment against the Plaintiff.

David Goodshoes
―――――――――――――――
David Goodshoes
Attorney for Defendants

Required Tasks:

Task 1: Prepare Plaintiff's Response to Defendant's Motion for Summary Judgment (the LexisNexis Web Course contains a form for the response that has been started for you).

Task 2: Prepare questions for Peter that might lead to additional helpful information for your case.

Practice Skills Utilized:

Skill 1: Legal analysis and writing

Skill 2: Strategic thinking

Estimated Time for Completion: Approximately 1-1 ½ hours

Level of Difficulty (1 to 5):

DO NOT PROCEED TO THE NEXT PAGE UNTIL YOU HAVE COMPLETED THE EXERCISE

SELF-ASSESSMENT

Required Tasks:

Task 1: Prepare Plaintiff's Response to Defendant's Motion for Summary Judgment.

Task 2: Prepare questions for Peter that might lead to additional helpful information for your case.

Practice Skills Utilized:

Skill 1: Legal analysis and writing

Skill 2: Strategic thinking

Task 1: **Prepare Plaintiff's Response to Defendant's Motion for Summary Judgment.**

Analysis/Writing: Your Response to Defendant's Motion for Summary Judgment should first have challenged the application of the *Hazelwood* standard. Is this really the type of curricular assignment that should be subject to *Hazelwood*? Especially when the guidelines for the project did not mention any prohibition on goods that might offend the political sensibilities of others? Couldn't this be argued to be almost pure political speech, as in *Tinker*, that shouldn't be regulated unless it "materially and substantially" interfered with school discipline?

Under the *Tinker* standard, do the undisputed facts demonstrate such a material and substantial disruption? Is Charlie becoming upset any worse than the warnings and wrecked math lesson described by Justice Black's *Tinker* dissent? Couldn't those students who were offended by Peter's card have simply averted their eyes or thrown it away? Should the "marketplace of ideas" be allowed to work in Classroom City, so that those who agreed with the message might "purchase" the product, and those who did not (such as Charlie) either refuse to "purchase" or obtain a "refund" for the product?

Even under the *Hazelwood* standard, is the ban on the political cards reasonably related to legitimate pedagogical interests? Is the interest in keeping other students from being offended a legitimate interest? Isn't provocative speech usually likely to offend? Does this mean that a school can outlaw all provocative ideas in any assigned project that encourages creativity?

Your response should have addressed most of the preceding questions. The best method to organize the response would be to first attack the application of *Hazelwood*, then explain why summary judgment was inappropriate under *Tinker*, and finally argue that, even under *Hazelwood*, summary judgment should be denied.

Task 2: **Prepare questions for Peter that might lead to additional helpful information for your case.**

Strategic Thinking: In dealing with a younger client like Peter, an ethical concern is that too much "suggestion" might lead to altered memories and the procurement of false testimony. As a result, instead of asking him whether the school unfairly allowed other products that might be described as political in nature, it might be better to have him discuss all the projects he could remember, and then you could follow up to obtain details on the arguably political projects to ensure the school was not discriminating based on the message expressed.

Similar care should be used to determine the extent to which school teachers and the administration had expressed contrary political views to Peter, whether politics were frequently discussed by other children at the school, and how the school had treated any analogous political controversies.

Chapter 8
GOVERNMENT SPEECH

INTRODUCTION

Government speech occurs when the government advances its own message in the First Amendment marketplace of ideas. Governmental officials or agencies frequently engage in expression in an attempt to garner public support for governmental policies. In other situations, the government funds or otherwise supports speech by private actors, but only on the condition that the expression of these private persons advances the government's position. Such viewpoint-based funding and support is authorized when the government is itself the speaker because the government is ultimately "accountable to the electorate and the political process for its advocacy. If the citizenry objects, newly elected officials later could espouse some different or contrary position." *Board of Regents v. Southworth*, 529 U.S. 217, 235 (2000). Government speech is thus not regulated by the judiciary under the free speech guarantee of the First Amendment, but instead is predominantly regulated by the people through the political process.

The distinction between government speech and private speech is therefore critical. Although sometimes this distinction is self-evident, such as when a governmental official expresses a view through governmentally controlled channels, in other instances, such as in governmental funding of private expression, the distinction is fuzzy. How much weight should be placed on the identity of the literal speaker? How important is governmental or private editorial control over the message at issue? Is the source of funding for the speech dispositive? Should the distinction between government and private speech depend on an objective standard focusing on whether the reasonable observer would attribute the speech to the government, a subjective standard relying on the underlying purposes of the expression, or both objective and subjective standards?

Because government speech as a distinct free speech concept has only recently been acknowledged by the courts, many of these issues have not been definitively resolved. As Justice Souter remarked, the government speech doctrine is "relatively new, and correspondingly imprecise." *Johanns v. Livestock Marketing Association*, 544 U.S. 550, 574 (2005) (Souter, J., dissenting). The Supreme Court held in *Johanns* that a promotional campaign for beef products was government speech when the Secretary of Agriculture exercised final approval authority over each word in the campaign, members of the Department of Agriculture participated in formulating the promotional proposals, the government established the overall message to be communicated, and the government funded the program through an assessment on cattle sales and importation. *Id.* at 561–62. But the existing decisions from the federal appellate courts on the weight to be afforded to such considerations often conflict, with some courts focusing on editorial control and other courts using a variety of factors.

Until the Supreme Court provides more guidance in the area, litigants and lower courts confront a challenge in deciding whether certain expression constitutes government speech. All that is certain is, if the expression is government speech, the government may exercise complete control over the message, without providing any support for opposing viewpoints.

EXERCISE 8:

Specialty license plates, which are available for purchase and contain a specialized design and slogan, are issued by almost every state. Many states have authorized more than a hundred different speciality plates, including ones for colleges and universities, military and veterans groups, civic and professional organizations, professional sports teams, public servants, and issue advocacy groups. Some examples include:

The state typically charges an extra $25–$50 per year for the plates, with the proceeds frequently split between the state treasury and some type of fund benefitting the private organization. Many states create the plates based on designs submitted by defined eligible institutions, which usually pay an application fee and provide either prepaid orders or evidence that a specified number of individuals will likely purchase the plates.

But this relatively open process in many states has led to litigation when requests for specialty plates are denied. As one example, some states have resisted a requested design by the Sons of Confederate Veterans that includes a Confederate flag. Other states have refused to issue a pro-choice specialty plate, even while offering a pro-life specialty plate. And certain organizations, such as the Ku Klux Klan, are usually entirely excluded from the process.

The courts have reached conflicting decisions regarding whether such specialty license plates are private speech or government speech. *Cf., e.g., Arizona Life Coalition, Inc. v. Stanton*, 515 F.3d 956, 965–68 (9th Cir. 2008) (private speech) & *Sons of Confederate Veterans, Inc. v. Commissioner of the Virginia Department of Motor Vehicles*, 288 F.3d 610, 621 (4th Cir. 2002) (private speech) *with ACLU of Tennessee v. Bredesen*, 441 F.3d 370, 375 (6th Cir. 2006) (government speech). If the specialty license plates are government speech, the state has no obligation to authorize plates with viewpoints with which it does not agree. But if the specialty plates are private speech, viewpoint discrimination would be forbidden, unless perhaps strict scrutiny could be satisfied.

You are a legislator in a state that does not currently have a specialty license plate program, but would like to develop such a program as a method to increase state revenues. The state wants to ensure that its license plates are government speech so that it can control the messages disseminated and will be less likely to have a lawsuit filed against it. How would you draft the legislation to make it as likely as possible that it will be viewed as government speech?

Required Tasks:

Task 1: Identify the factors that will make a judicial determination that the specialty plate program is government speech more likely.

Task 2: Draft a statutory description of the program that would be most likely to be viewed as government speech.

Practice Skills Utilized:

Skill 1: Legal analysis

Skill 2: Statutory drafting

Estimated Time for Completion: Approximately 1 ½ hours

Level of Difficulty (1 to 5):

Practice Tip: The LexisNexis Web Course contains links to relevant cases and offers multiple choice questions for review.

DO NOT PROCEED TO THE NEXT PAGE UNTIL YOU HAVE COMPLETED THE EXERCISE

SELF-ASSESSMENT

Required Tasks:

Task 1: Identify the factors that will make a judicial determination that the specialty plate program is government speech more likely.

Task 2: Draft a statutory description of the program that would be most likely to be viewed as government speech.

Practice Skills Utilized:

Skill 1: Legal analysis

Skill 2: Statutory drafting

Task 1: **Identify the factors that will make a judicial determination that the specialty plate program is government speech more likely.**

Legal Analysis: Although the weight of the factors for evaluating whether expression constitutes government speech is still in flux, it appears that, as observers become less likely to associate the speech with the state, the state's accountability for any message is diminished, and the more likely it becomes that the speech is private speech. *Cf. Planned Parenthood of South Carolina, Inc. v. Rose*, 361 F.3d 786, 799 (4th Cir. 2004) (Michael, J.). With respect to the plate program, then, the following considerations may offer guidance:

- The more that government opens up the program to a variety of different messages and slogans, the less likely it is that the plate program will be considered government speech.

- The more that government restricts the program to government-related messages or groups, such as veterans, judges, state employees, state universities and schools, the more likely it is that the plates will be considered government speech.

- The more that the message on the plate originates with the government, the more likely it is that the plate program will be considered government speech.

- The more that the government controls the process of proposing and issuing the specialty license plates, the more likely it is that the plate program will be considered government speech.

- The more editorial control the government exercises, the more likely it is that the plate program will be considered government speech.

Task 2: **Draft a statutory description of the program that would be most likely to be viewed as government speech.**

Statutory Drafting: A variety of approaches could be used in drafting the statutory program. Some ideas to consider include:

- Specifying only certain plates that can be issued, such as for departments, agencies, charities, or programs benefitting the state;
- Requiring any other plate design to be specifically authorized by implementing legislation describing the plate's relationship to state interests;
- Providing that the design of the plate should be made by the state, or at least with a committee including a number of state officials, with sufficient standards to guide the authorization and design process, including required identification markings, size of lettering, placement of symbols, and similar matters;
- Limiting the role of private groups to submitting a proposal for a plate; and
- Specifying the state has the final decision on each word of the message and the logo, and is to deny any plate design that is contrary to the public policy of the state.

Drafting the statute, however, can be quite a challenge, especially when trying to balance the need for precision with the necessary First Amendment constraints.

Chapter 9
FREEDOM OF EXPRESSIVE ASSOCIATION

INTRODUCTION

While the text of the First Amendment does not explicitly protect a right of expressive association, the freedom to associate for the purpose of advancing ideas and airing grievances is a necessary adjunct to freedom of speech. *NAACP v. Alabama ex rel. Patterson*, 357 U.S. 449, 460 (1958). Without the ability to gather with like-minded individuals to engage in First Amendment activity, the protected expressive rights would lose much of their practical significance. Thus, implicit within the other rights protected by the First Amendment is "a corresponding right to associate with others in pursuit of a wide variety of political, social, economic, educational, religious, and cultural ends." *Roberts v. United States Jaycees*, 468 U.S. 609, 623 (1984).

Because the freedom of expressive association is a correlative right, it arises in a variety of contexts. In some cases, the government attempts to compel a private association, such as the NAACP, to reveal the identify of its members, which the Supreme Court held is impermissible unless necessary to serve some compelling governmental interest. *NAACP*, 357 U.S. at 460–61. The government has also threatened public employees with termination unless they divulged the organizations to which they belonged, but this is likewise improper unless membership in the organization relates to employees' fitness and competency for their position. *Shelton v. Tucker*, 364 U.S. 479, 485–88 (1960). The government on other occasions seeks to regulate the internal conduct of private associations, including precluding the association from undertaking specified activities, penalizing the association in some manner for its conduct, or banning discrimination in the association's membership on the basis of sexual orientation, gender, race, religion or similar criteria. The association may then challenge such regulations as violating its right of expressive association, requiring the government to establish that any significant interference with the association's expression is necessary to serve a compelling governmental interest unrelated to the suppression of speech. *Boy Scouts of America v. Dale*, 530 U.S. 640, 648 (2000). The freedom of expressive association also provides protection for political parties, preventing the government from substantially burdening their associational rights unless strict scrutiny is satisfied. *California Democratic Party v. Jones*, 530 U.S. 567, 574–82 (2000).

Despite the number of ways in which the issue arises, strict scrutiny is only appropriate if the organization is an expressive association and the government has significantly interfered with its expression in some manner. Otherwise, a rational basis or reasonableness standard will be applied, which does not provide much protection. Thus, in these cases, the first issue an attorney must consider is whether the organization is an expressive association and how the organization's expressive rights have been burdened.

EXERCISE 9:

Your client, Bif Boyd, has been criminally charged with hazing. The indictment reads as follows:

IN THE 99th CRIMINAL JUDICIAL COURT
STATE OF MARSCH

STATE OF MARSCH	§	
	§	
v.	§	Violations of Penal Code § 33.03
	§	
BIF BOYD	§	

INDICTMENT

The Grand Jury charges:

Background:

1. The defendant, BIF BOYD ("Boyd"), is the fraternity pledge master of the Alpha Alpha Alpha male service fraternity at Mason College, a private university in Marsch. In this position, he arranges all events involving the provisional new members of the fraternity, referred to as "pledges."

2. Boyd heavily advertised an event on October 10 for the pledges of Alpha Alpha Alpha to clean the bear pits maintained by Mason College, posting fliers all around the campus encouraging students to watch the pledges perform "menial labor" by "cleaning the dung" of the campus mascots.

3. A significant crowd gathered on October 10 to watch the cleaning of the bear pits by the pledges. A number of members in the audience began heckling and tormenting the pledges mercilessly as they worked.

4. Several pledges asked Boyd if they could quit, but Boyd said that if they did so, they would not become full members of Alpha Alpha Alpha.

5. Bif then required the pledges to shout, "By serving others, we do the best for ourselves," while they worked.

6. One pledge, Heath Wimple, collapsed soon after being required to shout while working as he was being heckled by the members of the audience. He was taken to receive medical attention and diagnosed as having suffered from a combination of dehydration and elevated stress levels.

Count 1

7. The above-described actions constitute hazing under Marsch Penal Code § 33.03 (A)(2).

8. Boyd committed an intentional, knowing, or reckless act, on the campus of Mason College, that endangered the mental or physical health of Heath Wimple, by requiring him to continue to work at the bear pits and to shout during the bear pit clean-up if he wanted to become a full member of Alpha Alpha Alpha.

9. This physical activity subjected Heath Wimple to an unreasonable risk of harm and adversely affected his mental or physical health.

10. Boyd thereby engaged in hazing as prohibited by MPC § 33.03 (A)(2).

Count 2

8. The above-described actions constitute hazing under Marsch Penal Code § 33.03 (A)(4).

9. Boyd's intentional, knowing, or reckless act of requiring Heath Wimple to continue to work at the bear pits and to shout during the bear pit clean-up subjected Heath Wimple to extreme mental stress, shame, or humiliation, and adversely affected his mental health or dignity.

10. Boyd thereby engaged hazing as prohibited by MPC § 33.03 (A)(4).

DATED: October 19   A TRUE BILL

Judson Bend
District Attorney

David Donovan
Foreperson

Marsch Penal Code § 33.03—Hazing

(A) Hazing is any intentional, knowing, or reckless act, occurring on or off the campus of an educational institution, by one person alone or acting with others, directed against a student, that endangers the mental or physical health or safety of a student for the purpose of pledging, being initiated into, affiliating with, holding office in, or maintaining membership in any organization whose members are or include students at an educational institution. Hazing includes

(1) any type of physical brutality, such as whipping, beating, striking, branding, shocking, or similar activity;

(2) any type of physical activity, such as sleep deprivation, exposure to the elements, calisthenics, or other activity that subjects the student to an unreasonable risk of harm or that adversely affects the mental or physical health of the student;

(3) any activity involving consumption of food, liquid, alcoholic beverage, liquor, drug, or other substance which subjects the student to an unreasonable risk of harm or which adversely affects the mental or physical health of the student; or

(4) any activity that intimidates or threatens the student with ostracism, that subjects the student to extreme mental stress, shame, or humiliation, or that adversely affects the mental health or dignity of the student.

(B) A person commits an offense if the person:

(1) engages in hazing;

(2) solicits, encourages, directs, aids, or attempts to aid another in engaging in hazing;

(3) recklessly permits hazing to occur; or

(4) has firsthand knowledge of a specific hazing incident and fails to report that knowledge in writing to the dean of students or other appropriate official of the institution.

(C) Any person who commits the offense of hazing shall be guilty of a third-degree felony.

Additional Facts:

These are the additional facts provided to you by Bif. The philosophy of Alpha Alpha Alpha is that service to others is the mission of humans on Earth. Although there is no particular religious belief required by Alpha Alpha Alpha, all members must commit to its motto: "By serving others, we do the best for ourselves." New members of Alpha Alpha Alpha are selected through an extensive application and interview process to ensure a deeply ingrained desire for service. Once selected, the provisional new member becomes a "pledge" for six weeks and, during this time, must show his commitment to the service of others.

The last event of the six-week pledging period is the semi-annual cleaning of the campus bear pits, which is the home of Mason College's prior bear cub mascots once they become too large to be considered cubs. Before the cleaning, the bears are placed into their cages by their professional handlers. Then, the pledges of Alpha Alpha Alpha are brought into the bear pit to clean up the accumulated waste of the bears and any trash that has been deposited into the pit. The cleaning of the bear pits is a big campus event at Mason College, with students coming out to cheer (and sometimes jeer) the pledges as they commit their last act of service before becoming full fledged members of Alpha Alpha Alpha.

Bif posted the following flier everywhere around campus before the semi-annual bear cleaning event in order to disseminate the fraternity's message of service:

COME TO THE SEMI-ANNUAL BEAR PIT CLEANING

Sponsored by Alpha Alpha Alpha
"By serving others, we do the best for ourselves"

The Alpha Alpha Alpa pledges will perform the ultimate act of service — cleaning the dung of our mascots so that the bear pits can be enjoyed by all, alumni and students alike.

So come out and give our pledges some support as they perform this menial labor and show that through service we gain our best earthly rewards.

The crowd for the bear pit cleaning was, as Bif hoped, enormous. But the size of the crowd brought out many more hecklers than in years past, and a large, boisterous group of mostly business students barraged the pledges with a constant stream of demeaning torments while they were working. Some of the pledges wanted to quit because of the heckling, but Bif was energized, seeing this as an opportunity to illustrate the benefits of the Alpha Alpha Alpha philosophy, and he told the pledges to shout out as they worked the Alpha Alpha Alpha motto, "By serving others, we do the best for ourselves."

Unfortunately, though, one of the pledges, Heath Wimple, had a nervous breakdown as a result of the heckling and went to receive medical attention. Medical personnel reported the incident to Mason College and the district attorney's office. The district attorney, who was not fond of Mason College, brought the above-indictment against Bif for hazing based on the above-described activities.

Required Tasks:

Task 1: Draft a motion to dismiss the indictment on constitutional grounds (the LexisNexis Web Course contains a form for the motion that has been started for you).

Task 2: Prepare a list of any other information which would be relevant to the dismissal that needs to be developed.

Practice Skills Utilized:

Skill 1: Legal analysis

Skill 2: Motion drafting

Skill 3: Strategic thinking

Estimated Time for Completion: Approximately 1½ hours

Level of Difficulty (1 to 5):

**DO NOT PROCEED TO THE NEXT PAGE UNTIL YOU
HAVE COMPLETED THE EXERCISE**

SELF-ASSESSMENT

Required Tasks:

Task 1: Draft a motion to dismiss the indictment on constitutional grounds.

Task 2: Prepare a list of any other information which would be relevant to the dismissal that needs to be developed.

Practice Skills Utilized:

Skill 1: Legal analysis

Skill 2: Motion drafting

Skill 3: Strategic thinking

Task 1: **Draft a motion to dismiss the indictment on constitutional grounds.**

Legal Analysis: Your motion to dismiss will need to establish all the elements of an expressive association claim, as outlined in the introduction to this chapter. Did you first establish that Alpha Alpha Alpha was an expressive association? What makes it expressive? Is it enough that it has a motto and a philosophy regarding service to others? How important is it that Alpha Alpha Alpha is not engaged in commercial activities, but instead appears to be devoted to civic purposes?

Is the State of Marsch significantly interfering with Alpha Alpha Alpha's expression by applying MPC § 33.03 to Bif Boyd's activities as pledge master? Could the language of § 33.03(A)(2) arguably apply to any arduous service project performed by Alpha Alpa Alpha's pledges because such a project would constitute "physical activity" that "subjects the student to an unreasonable risk of harm or that adversely affects the mental or physical health of the student"? Could § 33.03(A)(4) apply to any service project that might be viewed as demeaning, under the reasoning that such a project would adversely affect the "dignity" of the student? Does the potential breadth of these provisions indicate that the State has significantly interfered with Alpha Alpha Alpha's service philosophy?

Does the government have a compelling governmental interest unrelated to the suppression of speech for this interference? Is the interest in preventing adverse effects on the mental or physical health of the student compelling and unrelated to the suppression of expression? How about the interest in protecting the student's "dignity" and preventing extreme "shame or humiliation"?

Do you have a better argument that, while the government may have at least some compelling governmental interests, that there are significantly less restrictive methods than articulated in MPC §§ 33.03(A)(2) & (4) to serve those interests? Could the statute prevent physical abuse and brutality without prohibiting as much "physical activity" (including calisthenics, practiced in gym classes across the land) and activities that adversely affect the "dignity" of the student? Were Bif's activities really the kind of actions that implicate the government's interests in preventing hazing?

Motion Drafting: In drafting your motion, remember the lessons you learned in your legal research and writing class. Use headings, be persuasive, and keep the argument as direct and concise as possible.

Task 2: **Prepare a list of any other information which would be relevant to the dismissal that needs to be developed.**

Strategic Thinking: Most of the relevant material that you needed for the dismissal motion was provided to you in the problem. But a few other pieces of information might have been helpful to develop. For example, would it have been useful to learn the types of service activities performed by members of Alpha Alpha Alpha and compare those activities to those expected of the pledges? If so, why? Would you have wanted to know whether any other Alpha Alpha Alpha pledges had had a similar breakdown? Would that have been relevant to your First Amendment defense? What other information would it have been useful to obtain?

Chapter 10
THE POLITICAL PROCESS AND THE FIRST AMENDMENT

INTRODUCTION

Political expression is at the core of the First Amendment. Yet the government has compelling reasons to regulate such expression in certain circumstances where it is necessary, for instance, to prevent actual corruption or the appearance of corruption in the political process. The difficulty is determining when laws governing political expression are indeed essential to supporting compelling governmental interests, rather than serving illegitimate concerns such as stifling dissident political expression or protecting incumbents from political rivals. The courts frequently must resolve these issues in cases brought by political parties, campaigns, and activists challenging laws that govern campaign finance and political speech.

The foundational campaign finance case is *Buckley v. Valeo*, 424 U.S. 1, 19–23 (1976), which distinguished contributions to a political candidate from political expenditures. While recognizing that caps on contributions somewhat restrict political communication, the Court reasoned that a reasonable contribution limit only marginally impacts the contributor's symbolic expression of support for the candidate. This marginal impact, the Court continued, is outweighed by the compelling governmental interests in reducing the probability of corruption and the appearance of corruption frequently inherent in inordinately generous campaign contributions. *Id.* at 26–28. In contrast, expenditures by a campaign or by independent groups have a closer relationship to political expression without the same connection to corruption. *Id.* at 44–58. As a result, the Court determined that a sufficient governmental interest did not support a financial cap on such expenditures. Thus, although those regulations necessary to serve a compelling governmental interest, such as reasonable contribution limits, are constitutional, those not serving similar compelling governmental interests, such as campaign expenditure limits, are invalid.

The same principle also applies to other aspects of governmental regulation of the political process, requiring heightened scrutiny of laws substantially infringing on the expressive or associational rights of voters or political parties. Sometimes strict scrutiny is satisfied, such as in *Burson v. Freeman*, 504 U.S. 191, 199–202 (1992) (Blackmun, J., plurality op.), which reasoned that compelling governmental interests in preventing voter intimidation and election fraud justified a ban on soliciting votes or displaying or distributing campaign literature within 100 feet of the entrance to a polling place. But in other instances, the Court has reasoned that strict scrutiny is not satisfied, such as in

Brown v. Hartlage, 456 U.S. 45, 58–62 (1982), which concluded that the state could not prohibit a county commissioner candidate from promising during his campaign to serve at a reduced salary, or *First National Bank of Boston v. Bellotti*, 435 U.S. 765, 878–95 (1978), which held that banks and business corporations could not be precluded from spending money to express their views on ballot initiatives and referenda.

Strict scrutiny also applies to the canons of judicial conduct that regulate the speech of judicial candidates in the approximately forty states that choose at least some of their judges through popular elections. The Supreme Court employed this heightened scrutiny in *Republican Party of Minnesota v. White*, 536 U.S. 765, 775–84 (2002), to invalidate the Minnesota Judicial Code of Conduct's prohibition on a judicial candidate announcing a view on a disputed legal or political issue that might come before the judge. The Supreme Court reasoned that this "announce clause," despite its enactment by a majority of the states, was not narrowly tailored to serve the government's asserted interest in impartiality. A judicial candidate's announcement of a view on an issue, the Court explained, does not impact the judge's ability to fairly dispense justice to the parties, nor would it be any more destructive of judicial open-mindedness than other acceptable avenues of expressing the same thought, such as books or written opinions.

The Court's holding in *White* led many states to hurriedly amend their own judicial conduct codes (links to some of these amended codes are provided on the LexisNexis Web Course). But the question of whether the amended codes satisfy the First Amendment has not been definitively resolved.

EXERCISE 10:

After the Supreme Court's decision in *Republican Party of Minnesota v. White*, 536 U.S. 765 (2002), the State of Mayfield revised the Mayfield Code of Judicial Conduct. As revised, the applicable portion of the Code provides:

> A judge or judicial candidate shall not:
>
> (1) make pledges or promises of conduct in office regarding pending or impending cases, specific classes of cases, specific classes of litigants, or specific propositions of law that would suggest to a reasonable person that the judge is predisposed to a probable decision in cases within the scope of the pledge.
>
> (2) make public comment about a pending or impending proceeding which may come before the court in which the judge serves or seeks to serve in a manner which suggests to a reasonable person the judge's probable decision on any particular case.
>
> (3) authorize the public use of his or her name endorsing another candidate for any public office. A judge or judicial candidate may, however, indicate support for a political party, attend political events, and express his or her views on political matters.

A law school classmate and good friend, Charlie Waterman, is running for an elected judicial position in Mayfield. Charlie has just received a questionnaire from a local civic group whose endorsements are often enough to ensure a candidate's victory. Charlie accordingly wants to provide as much information as possible in responding to the questionnaire, but is concerned that certain questions call for responses that may run afoul of the Mayfield Code of Judicial Conduct. Charlie has asked for your help in analyzing some of the questions under the Mayfield Code and, for any questions that may be prohibited, determining whether a First Amendment challenge to the application of the code provision may be warranted. The questions are as follows:

1. In interpreting the Mayfield Constitution, would you promise to strictly construct its text and original meaning, or would you interpret it as a living document that evolves over time?

2. Who are your judicial role models and why do you seek to emulate them?

3. Do you believe the right to trial by jury protected by the Mayfield Constitution has been eroded by the judiciary's increased willingness to enforce arbitration clauses in consumer contracts, employment agreements, and other contracts of adhesion?

4. Who will you support for President of the United States in the next election?

5. Would you promise to uphold all abortion laws unless binding precedent from the Supreme Court of the United States required the law's invalidation?

Required Tasks:

Task 1: After studying *White* again, prepare in outline form your opinions and supporting rationales regarding whether each question violates the Mayfield Code of Judicial Conduct and the likelihood of success for a First Amendment challenge to the Code provisions.

Task 2: Research whether answering some of the questions may require Charlie Waterman to be recused from certain cases involving those issues.

Practice Skills Utilized:

Skill 1: Judicial ethical rule analysis

Skill 2: Case analysis and legal reasoning

Skill 3: Legal research

Estimated Time for Completion: Approximately 2 hours

Level of Difficulty (1 to 5):

DO NOT PROCEED TO THE NEXT PAGE UNTIL YOU HAVE COMPLETED THE EXERCISE

SELF-ASSESSMENT

Required Tasks:

Task 1: After studying *White* again, prepare in outline form your opinions and supporting rationales regarding whether each question violates the Mayfield Code of Judicial Conduct and the likelihood of success for a First Amendment challenge to the Code provisions.

Task 2: Research whether answering some of the questions may require Charlie Waterman to be recused from certain cases involving those issues.

Practice Skills Utilized:

Skill 1: Judicial ethical rule analysis

Skill 2: Case analysis and legal reasoning

Skill 3: Legal research

Task 1: **Prepare in outline form your opinions and supporting rationales regarding whether each question violates the Mayfield Code of Judicial Conduct and the likelihood of success for a First Amendment challenge to the Code provisions.**

Rule Analysis:

Question 1

Is there a potential problem under the rules with question 1? Does the mere "promise" to adhere to a particular judicial philosophy violate the prohibition against pledges or promises, especially considering the specificity and predisposition requirements of the Code?

Question 2

Does question 2, seeking judicial role models, involve a pledge or promise, public comment on a pending or impending proceeding, or an endorsement? Could it possibly be a problem if one of Charlie's role models is a sitting judge who is running for reelection?

Question 3

Does the request to state a "belief" on the right to a trial by jury constitute a pledge or promise? Does it matter that the belief is predicated on a very specific issue, the enforcement of arbitration clauses in consumer contracts, employment agreements, and other contracts of adhesion?

Could answering this question possibly constitute a public comment on an impending case?

Question 4

Is stating who you will support for President the same as "endorsing" that person for public office? Could a candidate merely discuss his or her views of the political issues of the day, even though that would indirectly indicate support for a particular candidate?

Question 5

Is it a violation of the Code to promise to uphold all abortion laws in the absence of binding precedent? Would this suggest to a reasonable person that the judge is predisposed to a probable decision in abortion cases?

First Amendment: *White* held that regulations of a judicial candidate's speech must satisfy strict scrutiny. The Court recognized that a compelling governmental interest exists in preserving a judiciary free from bias or the appearance of bias for or against any party to a proceeding, and noted that there may be some desirability for a judge to have an open-mind, although the Court did not specifically determine whether open-mindedness was a compelling governmental interest. In any event, only those regulations that are narrowly tailored to serve these interests can be upheld as constitutional.

The issue of whether judicial open-mindedness is a compelling governmental interest is critical to the constitutionality of regulations that prohibit "pledges or promises" suggesting to a reasonable person that the judge is predisposed to a probable decision in cases within the scope of the pledge. At least one lower court has concluded that preserving an open-minded judiciary is a compelling governmental interest supporting an analogous pledge or promise clause. *Pennsylvania Family Institute, Inc. v. Celluci*, 521 F. Supp. 2d 351, 383–84 (E.D. Pa. 2007). But is "open-mindedness" really expected of judges? As an illustration, Justices Scalia and Thomas, based on their prior written opinions, will undoubtedly vote to uphold any legislative restriction on abortion that comes before the Supreme Court. What is the difference between a judge making such a commitment in a prior opinion versus in a political campaign? Is it more likely to be an impediment to an "open mind" that a promise or pledge was made in a campaign rather than in a previously authored judicial opinion on the issue? Does it matter if the judge is appointed or elected?

Is it arguably different if the pledge or promise, or even a public comment, is made regarding a pending or impending case and suggests the judge's probable decision in that particular case, which may implicate the compelling interest in protecting the due process rights of litigants by ensuring an impartial judge? Is such a judicial commitment to the outcome before the case begins more troublesome because the proceeding would thereby be rendered an exercise in futility, while a mere pledge or promise regarding an issue only makes transparent the candidate's predisposition on the issue?

Or, on the other hand, should all pledges or promises, whether on an issue or particular type of case, be viewed similarly? Can any pledge or promise be constitutionally prohibited because it indicates a commitment, while an announcement of views only indicates a predisposition? Is preventing a judicial commitment necessary to protect the legitimacy of the judicial branch, which, as the Supreme Court has noted in *Mistretta v. United States*, 488 U.S. 361, 407 (1989), "ultimately depends on its reputation for impartiality and nonpartisanship"?

What governmental interest supports the ban against a judge publicly endorsing another candidate for political office? Such a ban may be viewed as necessary to ensure judicial impartiality and to prevent the inappropriate use of the judiciary for partisan purposes. But, even assuming that these are compelling governmental purposes, is the regulation underinclusive to serve such purposes when a judge or judicial candidate may indicate support for a political party, attend political events, express his or her views on political matters, and contribute financially to political campaigns?

Even if the regulations are facially valid, can it be argued that the regulations cannot be constitutionally applied to the submitted questions? Assuming that the Code prevents a judicial candidate from answering the fourth and fifth questions, does Charlie have an argument that the application of the regulations to these particular questions is not narrowly tailored to serve a compelling governmental interest? Wouldn't a litigant in an abortion case, for example, prefer to know that a judge was predisposed to rule in a certain way, rather than the judge hiding such a predisposition, such that there might be some chance that the judge would recuse?

Task 2: **Research whether answering some of the questions may require Charlie Waterman to be recused from certain cases involving those issues.**

Legal Research: Due process guarantees a "fair trial in a fair tribunal" without "actual bias ... or interest in the outcome" of the litigation. *Bracy v. Gramley*, 520 U.S. 899, 904–05 (1997). This prohibits a judge from presiding who has a financial interest in the outcome of the case, *see, e.g., Tumey v. Ohio*, 273 U.S. 510, 523 (1927), who has been involved in the case in an accusatory role, *see, e.g., In re Muchison*, 349 U.S. 133, 137 (1955), or who has an actual bias or an intolerable risk of actual bias either for or against a particular party. *See, e.g., Caperton v. A.T. Massey Coal Co.*, 129 S. Ct. 2252, 2263 (2009); *Johnson v. Mississippi*, 403 U.S. 212, 215–16 (1971).

These precedents might also support an argument that pledges, promises, and public comments that suggest a judge's probable disposition of a case violate the due process rights of the litigants. Even if this argument was not ultimately successful, though, the states are permitted to exceed the minimum guarantees of due process in promulgating recusal standards. Thus, as Justice Kennedy discussed in his concurrence in *White*, a method for the states to protect judicial "integrity" and a "respect" for the courts is adopting "recusal standards more rigorous than due process requires, and censur[ing] judges who violate these standards." 536 U.S. at 793–94 (Kennedy, J., concurring). Many states in fact have adopted canons based on the ABA Model Code of Judicial Conduct, which prohibits a judge from presiding when "the judge's impartiality might reasonably be questioned." Under these canons, numerous state courts and lower federal courts have required the recusal of a judge for prior promises, pledges, or comments that prejudge the merits of a particular case. As a result, Charlie should be advised to carefully consider, for instance, whether answering the third and fifth questions may lead to future recusal motions and disciplinary complaints if such motions are denied.

Chapter 11
THE NEWSGATHERING FUNCTION AND FREEDOM OF THE PRESS

INTRODUCTION

In addition to the right to publish newsworthy information, the press has argued that the First Amendment protects the functional ability to gather news. This claim has arisen in two separate contexts. First, the press has argued that the First Amendment operates as a shield that protects its members from having to disclose the identity of confidential sources or the information obtained from them. Second, the press has sought to use the First Amendment as a sword to gain access to people, places, and proceedings otherwise off-limits to the public.

The Supreme Court has recognized that "without some protection for seeking the news, freedom of the press could be eviscerated." Yet newsgathering itself is not afforded absolute constitutional protection. Under *Branzburg v. Hayes*, 408 U.S. 665 (1972), for example, a journalist who refuses to testify about a confidential informant in response to a grand jury subpoena could be held in contempt of court, unless the subpoena is issued to harass the reporter or seeks information beyond what is relevant or material to a grand jury investigation. Nor can the press claim absolute immunity when served with a validly executed search warrant or a request for pretrial discovery in a civil case. According to the Court, the need for disclosure in these circumstances is said to outweigh any resulting burden on newsgathering.

The Court has also declined to afford the press a First Amendment "special right of access" beyond what is available to the public generally. Under this rule, reporters have been denied permission to inspect private areas of a prison facility, conduct face to face interviews with selected prisoners, or copy tape recordings used as evidence in a criminal trial. *See e.g., Pell v. Procunier*, 417 U.S. 817 (1974), *Saxbe v. Washington Post Co.*, 417 U.S. 843 (1974). In limited circumstances, however, a presumptive right of access attaches when "experience and logic" dictates that the proceeding should be open to the public. *Richmond Newspapers, Inc. v. Virginia*, 448 U.S. 555 (1980). Criminal trials, preliminary hearings, and juror voir dire fall into this category, based on an unbroken history of public access and the need to foster public trust in the criminal justice system. These proceedings can only be closed on a case by case basis, upon an explicit finding that closure is narrowly tailored to serve a compelling interest. *See Press Enterprise Co. v. Superior Court*, 464 U.S. 501 (1984); *Globe Newspapers v. Superior Court*, 457 U.S. 596 (1982). Lower federal and state courts have also applied the "experience and logic" test to determine whether the public, and by default the press, has a right to access civil trials, administrative hearings, agency records, and disciplinary proceedings.

Practice Tip: Though the Supreme Court has declined to recognize an absolute privilege rooted in the First Amendment, a qualified privilege exists in some jurisdictions. A majority of states have enacted shield statutes to regulate the circumstances under which a reporter can be compelled to testify or to limit the types of evidence that can be seized from the press in response to a warrant. Other states have adopted some form of reporter's privilege under the common law. Some lower courts even interpret *Branzburg* as establishing a qualified privilege that applies unless there is a compelling need for disclosing highly relevant information that cannot be obtained elsewhere. Similarly, statutes and administrative regulations may provide a right of access where one is not constitutionally required.

EXERCISE 11:

You represent Alicia Copeland, a reporter with THE NEW VALLEY TIMES, who broke a story on a secret government rendition program. She is seeking advice on a number of issues regarding a government investigation of the program. After reading the article below, how do you advise Copeland in the following situations:

Part 1

Copeland is served with a subpoena to testify and produce documents to the grand jury (copied below). Draft a motion to quash that would protect Copeland from having to appear before the grand jury. In addition to any constitutional arguments, note that under Rule 17(c)(2) of the Federal Rules of Criminal Procedure, a judge may quash or modify a subpoena for documents "if compliance would be unreasonable or oppressive."

Part 2

Following Copeland's interview with Dumsfeld regarding the CIA program, he incidentally mentioned his plans to run for President. If Dumsfeld is fired from his present job after his supervisor reads about the plan in Copeland's article, can he recover damages from her in a civil suit? What must you ask Copeland in order to answer this question?

Part 3

As a legislative aid in a state that has not enacted a reporter's shield statute, you are asked to draft a bill that strikes an appropriate balance between the needs of a free press and equally important alternative objectives. What does your proposal look like? Referring back to THE NEW VALLEY TIMES article may bring a number of issues into focus. Pay particular attention to the following considerations and be prepared to defend the specifics of your proposal:

- How will your statute define "reporter?"
- What type of information can a reporter keep confidential?
- Are there any requests that a reporter must respond to?
- Does the privilege apply in other circumstances?
- What type of showing, if any, is required to overcome the privilege?

Part 4

In addition to the secret rendition program, Copeland learns that deportation proceedings have been initiated against more than 100 foreign nationals allegedly involved in a human trafficking ring linked to organized crime. Copeland is suspicious of the allegations and decided to attend the deportation hearing to investigate. When she arrives at court, she learns that the Chief Immigration Judge has decided that any deportation proceeding that involves a "heightened security risk" as determined by the Department of Justice will be conducted in secret without access by the press or members of the public. That morning, the Department of Justice had declared that deportation proceedings involving charges of organized crime, like the one Copeland planned to attend, present a "heightened security risk." Copeland wants your advice on whether she has a First Amendment right to attend the proceedings.

Research applicable case law to determine whether Copeland can challenge the closure decision. Your results should yield at least two relevant Supreme Court cases and two lower court cases. How do you use these cases to support or distinguish Copeland's claim? What additional facts will help you better assess the claim?

Required Tasks:

Task 1: Draft a Motion to Quash the Grand Jury Subpoena (the LexisNexis Web Course contains a form for the motion that has been started for you).

Task 2: Investigate additional facts to determine whether Copeland can be held liable for disclosing Dumsfeld's plans to run for President.

Task 3: Draft a proposed reporter's privilege statute that balances the interest in disclosure against the need to protect confidential information.

Task 4: Research case law to determine whether Copeland has a right to access a closed deportation proceeding.

Practice Skills Utilized:

Skill 1: Legal analysis

Skill 2: Motion drafting

Skill 3: Factual investigation

Skill 4: Computer research

Estimated Time for Completion: Approximately 2 1/2 hours

Level of Difficulty (1 to 5):

THE NEW VALLEY TIMES

The news you need, when you need it. Since 1947.

Classified Documents Confirm Prisoner Renditions

DOJ Begins Investigation

by Alicia Copeland

A classified government report obtained by the New Valley Times confirms that over 100 individuals detained by the CIA in the war on terrorism were tortured by foreign intelligence agents after being transferred to prisons overseas. The report provides further proof of a secret rendition program that first came to light in 2005.

The prisoners were suspected of having ties to al Qaeda, but the CIA did not have enough evidence to charge them with a crime, an agent familiar with the program said. The President ordered them transferred to countries known to condone torture after routine CIA interrogations failed to produce any tangible leads. The rendition program was set to expire last year but another agent, who spoke on condition of anonymity, said the CIA is still sending prisoners to "torture-camps."

Several military and government oversight blogs are making the same claim. One blog, operated by former Defense Secretary Ronald Dumsfeld, says the President used private pilots to transfer prisoners hoping to limit the involvement of military personnel she knew would oppose the program. Dumsfeld, who previously defended the use of "any means available" to extract information from potential terrorists, now says he disagrees with the Administration's tactics. It's likely that Dumsfeld will take additional steps to distance himself from the current Administration given his plans to run for President in the upcoming election.

The Department of Justice is investigating the existence of the rendition program and whether the treatment of detainees in federal custody violated international law. It also hopes to determine whether government officials unlawfully disclosed classified information about top secret programs.

United States District Court
District of Acadia

TO: Alicia Copeland   Subpoena To Testify
                                  Before Grand Jury

Subpoena for:

Person [x]   Documents or
                 Objects [x]

YOU ARE HEREBY COMMANDED to appear before the Grand Jury of the United States District Court at the place, date, and time specified below.

PLACE	COURTROOM, DATE AND TIME
U.S. District Court	Grand Jury Room 497
1 Federal Plaza	4/24
Leland, Acadia 32993	10:00 a.m.

YOU ARE ALSO COMMANDED to provide testimony as requested on the following:

1. How you came to possess the classified government report described in the New Valley Times article *Classified Documents Confirm Prisoner Rendition*.

2. The identity of persons interviewed for the article, including but not limited to the person who reported to you that the "CIA did not have enough evidence to charge [the detainees] with a crime," and that "the CIA is still sending prisoners to 'torture camps'."

3. Any and all information related to the existence of a secret rendition program operated by the CIA.

YOU ARE ALSO COMMANDED to bring with you the following documents:

4. Any and all documents you relied on in the course of researching, drafting and revising the above referenced article.

5. Any and all documents relating to conversations you had with Ronald Dumsfeld, former Defense Secretary of the United States.

This subpoena shall remain in effect until you are granted leave to depart by the court or by an officer acting on behalf of the court.

MAGISTRATE JUDGE OR CLERK OF COURT	)))	DATE: 3/19
Janice L. Rodriguez, Clerk of Courts	)	
(By) Deputy Clerk	))	
S.F. Kurtz	)	
This subpoena is issued on application of the United States of America	)))	Attorney Name and Contact
K. Bradelman United States Attorney	))))	K. Bradelman Department of Justice 15 Victory Street Leland, Acadia 32993

DO NOT PROCEED TO THE NEXT PAGE UNTIL YOU HAVE COMPLETED THE EXERCISE

SELF-ASSESSMENT
Part 1

Task 1: **Draft a Motion to Quash the Grand Jury Subpoena.**

Motion Drafting: Refer to Skills & Values Chapter 11, LexisNexis Web Course: Motion to Quash

Legal Analysis: *Branzburg* holds that the First Amendment does not provide an absolute exemption for a reporter who is served with a subpoena to appear before a grand jury. So long as the subpoena is not oppressive or abusive, a reporter can be held in contempt for refusing to comply.

However, *Branzburg* has been interpreted by a number of lower courts as establishing a qualified privilege. Though the rules vary by jurisdiction, the privilege generally applies unless the government can show that: (1) the information is clearly relevant to a specific probable violation of law; (2) the information cannot be obtained by alternative means; and (3) there is a compelling and overriding interest in the information.

Consider the following as you determine whether there is a basis to quash the subpoena for each category of information requested:

1. How you came to possess the classified government report described in the New Valley Times article *Classified Documents Confirm Prisoner Rendition*.

   Under a narrow reading of *Branzburg*, Copeland has no protection for failing to comply with the subpoena under the First Amendment. What if a Federal Reporter's Privilege Act adopted the framework articulated in Justice Stewart's dissent in *Branzburg*?

   Does it matter if Copeland obtained the report from someone who disclosed it to her without authorization, or whether Copeland herself obtained the report illegally (did she hack a government website, or conspire to violate national security laws)?

2. The identity of persons interviewed for the article, including but not limited to the person who reported to you that the "CIA did not have enough evidence to charge [the detainees]

with a crime," and that "the CIA is still sending prisoners to 'torture camps'."

This request seeks the identity of at least two known informants, but the article only describes one of them as a confidential source. Neither source is protected under a narrow reading of *Branzburg*. Would either be protected under a Federal Reporter's Privilege Act that follows Justice Stewart's dissent?

Could Copeland be forced to disclose sources she consulted during her investigation but did not reference in the article?

3. Any and all information related to the identity of persons involved in a secret rendition program operated by the CIA.

Carefully review the article. How strong is the government's interest in obtaining this information from Copeland? Does the ability to obtain the information through another means mitigate the need to compel disclosure?

4. Any and all documents you relied on in the course of researching, drafting and revising the above referenced article.

Is there a basis for quashing this request under the proposed federal statute? Is there a basis to quash under *Branzburg* itself? Is there a legitimate need for "any and all documents" a reporter consulted for a particular article, or is this request overly burdensome?

5. Any and all documents relating to conversations you had with Ronald Dumsfeld, former Defense Secretary of the United States.

This item narrows the request to documents relating to conversations with Dumsfeld, but again, can you argue that the request is overly burdensome or otherwise not legitimate?

Part 2

Task 2: **Investigate additional facts to determine whether Copeland can be held liable for disclosing Dumsfeld's plans to run for President.**

Legal Analysis: Whether Dumsfeld can recover damages could depend on whether Copeland promised not to reveal his intent to run for President. *Cohen v. Cowles Media Co.*, 501 U.S. 663 (1991), allowed recovery under a theory of promissory estoppel where the reporter broke a promise not to disclose the identity of a source who provided confidential information. Is *Cohen* applicable here?

Part 3

Task 3: **Draft a proposed reporter's privilege statute that balances the interest in disclosure against the need to protect confidential information.**

Legal Drafting: How did you define "reporter?" Consider these alternatives:

- persons who maintain a living by reporting the news
- retired journalists
- student journalists
- bloggers
- writers subject to professional oversight or journalistic standards

What type of information can a reporter keep confidential? What about:

- information acquired in the process of preparing a report for public broadcast
- information acquired for student newspapers or blogs
- only information obtained upon a promise of confidentiality

Are there any requests that a reporter must respond to? Would the privilege apply to requests for information that are:

- authorized by any court or law enforcement official
- made in pursuance of any criminal investigation
- made as part of an investigation into certain crimes
- made as part of an investigation into past crimes
- made as part of an effort to prevent future crimes

Does the privilege apply in other circumstances, such as when:

- the initial disclosure is itself illegal (the informant is a government agent who illegally discloses the identity of an undercover agent)
- the subpoena is issued to a third party, such as a telephone company or internet service provider, that maintains a record of customer communications (including members of the press) in the normal course of business

What type of showing, if any, is required to overcome the privilege?

- must the reporters establish the privilege, or the government establish that the privilege does not apply
- that the information cannot be obtained through other means
- might exigent circumstances justify disclosure even when the information can be obtained elsewhere

Part 4

Task 4: **Research case law to determine whether Copeland has a right to access a closed deportation proceeding.**

Computer Research: Your research should have led you to four cases:

Richmond Newspapers v. Virginia, 448 U.S. 555 (1980) (holding criminal trials presumptively open to the public and the press).

Globe Newspaper Co. v. Superior Court, 457 U.S. 596 (1982) (invalidating mandatory closure statute while recognizing judge's discretion to close proceeding where "strict scrutiny" is satisfied).

Detroit Free Press v. Ashcroft, 303 F.3d 681 (6th Cir. 2002) (invalidating directive that requires closure of deportation proceeding absent showing of particularized compelling need in each case).

New Jersey Media Group v. Ashcroft, 308 F.3d 198 (3d Cir. 2002) (upholding blanket closure of deportation proceedings on national security grounds).

Because the press has no special right of access beyond what is given to the public, you must first determine whether deportation proceedings share the characteristics of a criminal trial that led the Court in *Richmond Newspapers* to hold that such proceedings are presumptively open to the public. If so, the government bears a heavy burden of justifying the closure under the strict scrutiny standard articulated in *Globe Newspaper Co.*

Did the closure directive meet this standard, and if not, do the circumstances of the case warrant deference? To answer this question consider the analysis offered in *Detroit Free Press* and *New Jersey Media Group*, where the Sixth and Third Circuits reached different conclusions on whether deportation proceedings could be summarily closed to the press. Pay attention to the following factors, and determine whether or not they favor Copeland's right to access the proceedings:

- Immigration courts are established under Article II rather than Article III where the right to a public trial applies under the Sixth Amendment. Did Article III play a role in the determination that criminal trials are presumptively open?

- The proceedings involve accusations of organized criminal activity. Does this liken the case to *New Jersey Media Group* where national security concerns took precedence?

- The directive does not state whether a transcript of the proceeding will be available. Is this relevant?

Chapter 12
THE ESTABLISHMENT CLAUSE

INTRODUCTION

Lawyers who practice in a variety of areas are likely to encounter an Establishment Clause problem at some point in their career. Lawyers who work for public interest organizations represent clients on both sides of the church-state controversy. Organizations like the American Civil Liberties Union, Americans United For Separation of Church and State, and The American Center for Law and Justice have played a major role in shaping Establishment Clause jurisprudence at the Supreme Court through direct client representation or amicus briefs submitted in noteworthy cases. The relationship between lawmakers and public interest lawyers is not always adversarial, however. Government officials often seek the advice of public interest attorneys to ensure that proposed or existing policies and procedures meet constitutional standards.

Establishment Clause cases have also been litigated by lawyers at every level of government. Attorneys with the Department of Justice, for instance, are not only responsible for prosecuting violations of the nation's laws, but defending the constitutionality of laws that are challenged in court. The Religious Land Use and Institutionalized Persons Act, Individuals With Disabilities in Education Act, and Elementary and Secondary Education Act are just three of the many federal statutes that have been challenged on Establishment Clause grounds. *See Cutter v. Wilkinson*, 544 U.S. 709 (2005); *Mitchell v. Helms*, 530 U.S. 793 (2000); *Zobrest v. Catalina Foothills School Dist.*, 509 U.S. 1 (1993). Establishment Clause challenges to state or local government action are also common, including challenges to public religious displays, school prayers, or curriculum requirements that mandate the teaching of creationism or "intelligent design" in public school. *See, e.g., Wallace v. Jaffree*, 472 U.S. 38 (1985); *Abington v. Schempp*, 374 U.S. 203 (1963); *Engel v. Vitale*, 370 U.S. 421 (1962); *Croft v. Texas,* 562 F.3d 735 (5th Cir. 2009); *Kitzmiller v. Dover Area School Dist.*, 400 F. Supp. 2d 707 (M.D. Pa. 2005). Attorneys in private practice often handle these cases alongside government lawyers.

It can be especially difficult to litigate an Establishment Clause claim because the applicable law is in a state of flux. *Lemon v. Kurtzman*, 403 U.S. 602 (1971), the seminal Establishment Clause case, takes into account the purpose, effect, and level of government entanglement with religion, but has been roundly criticized by individual members of the Court for failing to accommodate the historical role of religion in public life. Though *Lemon* has not been overruled, the Court has declined to apply it in some Establishment Clause cases while continuing to apply it in others. *Compare McCreary County v. ACLU*, 545 U.S. 844 (2005) with *Van Orden v. Perry*, 545 U.S. 677 (2005).

Because of dissatisfaction with *Lemon*, different constitutional standards have been applied in certain types of cases. Public funding cases have been analyzed under the doctrine of "neutrality," which enables religious organizations to participate in government programs on the same terms as private organizations. *See, e.g.*, *Zelman v. Simmons-Harris*, 536 U.S. 639 (2002). Public religious displays, curriculum requirements, and student-initiated prayers have been subject to an "endorsement" test that asks whether a reasonable observer would believe that the government has either approved or disapproved of religion in a way that makes adherence relevant to a person's "standing in the community." *See Lynch v. Donnelly*, 465 U.S. 668, 687 (1984) (O'Connor, J., concurring). The "coercion test" has also been applied to these situations, however. That approach allows the government to accommodate individual religious preferences so long as it does not directly or indirectly coerce participation from non-adherents. *See, e.g.*, *Lee v. Weisman*, 505 U.S. 577, 592–93 (1992).

Practice Tip: Asking whether a particular statute or regulation reflects a government "endorsement" or "coerces" non-adherents to participate in a religious exercise may be another way of asking whether the challenged law has either the "purpose" or "effect" of establishing religion. These tests are in fact a product of the criticism directed at *Lemon*. But *Lemon* has not been overruled, at least not yet, so don't forget to invoke that case when litigating an Establishment Clause claim.

THE ESTABLISHMENT CLAUSE

EXERCISE 12:

You work for a non-profit advocacy organization and have been asked to testify at an upcoming legislative hearing on whether either of two proposed amendments to a moment of silence statute would, if enacted, violate the Establishment Clause. Both proposals are reprinted below. Italicized text indicates an addition to the previous law; a strike-through indicates a deletion.

Draft an outline of the points you will raise during your testimony, citing relevant case law.

Required Tasks:

Task 1: Identify case law relevant to the constitutionality of a classroom moment of silence.

Task 2: Analyze whether either of the two proposals would violate the Establishment Clause (the LexisNexis Web Course contains clean copies of the proposals without italics or strikeouts).

Practice Skills Utilized:

Skill 1: Case research

Skill 2: Critical reasoning

Estimated Time for Completion: Approximately 45 minutes

Level of Difficulty (1 to 5):

Proposal 1:

Teachers shall reserve one minute at the start of each school day for a period of reflection *and reverence* during which time the teacher ~~may~~ *shall*:

(a) *Lead students in a recitation of the Pledge of Allegiance in accordance with Title 4, section 4 of the United States Code.*

~~(a)~~ *(b)* Instruct students to spend the *remaining* time independently in a ~~silent~~ moment of prayer *or meditation*.

Proposal 2:

Teachers shall reserve one minute at the start of each school day for a period of reflection *and reverence* during which time the teacher ~~may~~ *shall*:

(a) ~~Instruct students to spend the time independently in a silent moment of prayer.~~

(a) *Lead students in a recitation of the Pledge of Allegiance in accordance with Title 4, section 4 of the United States Code.*

(b) *Inform students of their constitutional right to pray in school, and lead willing students who voluntarily choose to participate in a moment of silent prayer.*

DO NOT PROCEED TO THE NEXT PAGE UNTIL YOU HAVE COMPLETED THE EXERCISE

SELF-ASSESSMENT

Required Tasks:

Task 1: Identify case law relevant to the constitutionality of a classroom moment of silence.

Task 2: Analyze whether either of the two proposals would violate the Establishment Clause.

Practice Skills Utilized:

Skill 1: Case research

Skill 2: Critical reasoning

Task 1:	**Identify case law relevant to the constitutionality of a classroom moment of silence.**
Case Research:	There is no question that students cannot be forced to pray in a public school. *Engel v. Vitale*, 370 U.S. 421 (1962), struck down a New York state requirement that schools begin each day with a prayer to "Almighty God." *Abington v. Schempp*, 374 U.S. 203 (1963), voided a Pennsylvania requirement that teachers start the day by reading "ten verses from the Holy Bible."
	Whether a moment of silence statute violates the Constitution even when students are not forced to pray is another question. The Supreme Court addressed the issue in *Wallace v. Jaffree*, 472 U.S. 38 (1985), finding Alabama's moment of silence policy unconstitutional under the purpose prong of *Lemon v. Kurtzman*, 403 U.S. 602 (1971). *Lemon*, of course, has been roundly criticized by a number of Justices and though the decision has not been overruled, a court today could very well borrow from other Establishment Clause cases and ask whether the challenged policy "endorses" religion or merely "accommodates" personal beliefs. *See, e.g., Lynch v. Donnelly*, 465 U.S. 668, 687 (O'Connor, J., concurring).
Task 2:	**Analyze whether either of the two proposals would violate the Establishment Clause.**
Critical Reasoning:	Proposal 1 allows students to meditate where previously they were only allowed to pray - essentially the converse of what happened in *Wallace*. Does this neutralize the risk of religious endorsement or coercion? What if lawmakers adopt the proposal in order to avoid a constitutional

challenge, but still want students to pray? Does the text tell you whether this is the case?

Moreover, though it provides an opportunity for meditation, the proposal deletes the reference to *silent* prayer. Does *Wallace* even apply if students can pray aloud in the classroom, or should you look to *Engel* and *Schempp* instead?

Proposal 2 raises a similar concern. Teachers here direct the exercise, but lead only *willing* students who choose to participate in a moment of *silent* prayer. Is this less problematic than a vocal prayer students initiate on their own? Is it coercive to students who do not want to pray? Before answering these questions you would want to look at cases involving school prayer in other contexts. *See, e.g., Santa Fe Independent School District v. Doe*, 530 U.S. 290 (2000). In our scenario, teachers are also required to inform students of their right to pray. Is that significant?

Finally, what do you make of the additional requirement in either proposal that students pledge the flag?

Chapter 13
THE FREE EXERCISE CLAUSE

INTRODUCTION

The Free Exercise Clause comes into play when a legal obligation conflicts with the requirements of a given faith. Consider this: should a prohibition on underage drinking apply at a Catholic mass where adherents sip wine as a symbolic representation of the blood of Christ? Should Jews who are not of age be prohibited from drinking wine during the Passover Seder, Purim celebration, or Sabbath ritual? Wine may be a sacred part of these religious ceremonies, but that does not discount the state's interest in controlling underage drinking. Laws such as these prohibit adherents from participating in rituals that are required by their religion. Do they violate the Free Exercise Clause?

What happens in the event of a constitutional conflict? A law that seeks to protect one person's right to equal protection or due process may interfere with another person's right to free exercise. Could a property owner be forced to rent an apartment to a gay or lesbian couple if she believes that doing so is contrary to the laws of God? Must a doctor perform an abortion or a pharmacist fill a birth control prescription against the dictates of their religion?

A challenge to any of these laws would present three common issues: (1) whether the plaintiff has established a genuinely held religious belief; (2) whether the law substantially burdens an exercise of that belief; and (3) what standard of review applies if there is a substantial burden on religion.

The Free Exercise Clause only protects sincerely held religious beliefs, as opposed to other important, though non-religious, personal convictions. The inquiry is largely subjective, and is not concerned with whether the religious belief is reasonable or accepted by mainstream organized faiths. *Thomas v. Review Bd. Ind. Empl. Sec.*, 450 U.S. 707 (1981); *United States v. Ballard*, 322 U.S. 78 (1944). Moreover, the Free Exercise Clause does not apply to a law that simply makes it more difficult to practice religion. In order to trigger constitutional scrutiny, the law must "substantially burden," or effectively coerce, a religious adherent into violating a sincerely held belief. *Lyng v. Northwest Indian Cemetery Protective Ass'n*, 485 U.S. 439 (1988).

Whether such a law is unconstitutional, however, depends on the standard of review that applies in a given case. *Employment Division v. Smith*, 494 U.S. 872 (1990), held that a neutral, generally applicable criminal law that substantially burdens religion will be upheld so long as it is "reasonable." *Cf. Jacobson v. Massachusetts*, 197 U.S. 11 (1905) (rejecting Equal Protection Clause challenge to mandatory state smallpox vaccine). This standard makes it difficult for plaintiffs to establish a constitutionally based exemption from a generally applicable law because all presumptions favor the government.

But *Smith* did not overrule *Hobbie v. Unemployment Appeals Commission*, 480 U.S. 136 (1987) or *Sherbert v. Verner*, 374 U.S. 398 (1963), where the Court ruled in favor of religious adherents who were disqualified from receiving unemployment benefits after refusing to work on their Sabbath. Nor did it overrule *Wisconsin v. Yoder*, 406 U.S. 205 (1972), which enjoined the enforcement of a compulsory education law against religious adherents. Strict scrutiny applied in these cases, which meant the government had to prove that the law served a compelling objective that could not be achieved in an alternative, less burdensome way. Three years after *Smith* was decided, *Church of the Lukumi Babalu Aye, Inc. v. Hialeah*, 508 U.S. 520 (1993), held that strict scrutiny also applied to laws that purposefully discriminate against religion.

Further complicating matters is the tension that exists between the two religion clauses of the First Amendment. In some scenarios, the government's effort to avoid an Establishment Clause violation risks a violation of the Free Exercise Clause, as when government officials prohibit certain religious practices in public school. In *Locke v. Davey*, 540 U.S. 712 (2004), Chief Justice Rehnquist announced that there must be "room for play in the joints" between the religion clauses, and that some state actions might be "permitted by the Establishment Clause, but not required by the Free Exercise Clause." There is no bright line rule for resolving these complicated cases, however.

Practice Tip: Lawmakers can avoid some of these conflicts legislatively. In response to *Smith*, Congress passed the Religious Freedom and Restoration Act, which prohibits any substantial burden on religion unless it is the least restrictive means of furthering a compelling interest. Although *Boerne v. Flores*, 521 U.S. 507 (1997), subsequently held that RFRA was an unconstitutional restriction on generally applicable state laws, RFRA nonetheless remains valid as a restriction on generally applicable federal laws. See *Gonzales v. O Centro Espirita Beneficente Uniao do Vegetal*, 546 U.S. 418 (2006). Moreover, a number of states have passed their own 'mini-RFRA' statutes, and the federal government has passed the Religious Land Use and Institutionalized Persons Act, which subjects municipal zoning laws and prison regulations that substantially burden religion to strict scrutiny analysis.

Other statutes also seek to balance free exercise rights with competing interests. Title VII of the Civil Rights Act prohibits various types of employment discrimination but does not apply to certain hiring decisions that would violate the employer's religious obligations. The Fair Housing Act prohibits discrimination in the rental of housing units, but includes a limited exemption for religious organizations and does not even apply to small apartment owners who live in close proximity to tenants. Similarly, most underage drinking and controlled substances laws accommodate at least some religious sacraments. Religious convictions are also being considered as more states move to extend legal protection to gay, lesbian and transgendered persons. Without a statutory or regulatory exemption, however, the Free Exercise Clause may come into play, leaving courts to strike a difficult balance between competing interests.

EXERCISE 13:

The state of Astoria enacted a statute that requires females between the ages of 9 and 11 to receive a vaccine against the Human Papilloma Virus [HPV] before they can enroll in public school. The statute was passed in response to a spike in adult onset cervical cancer which scientists believe can be caused by a prior HPV infection. The virus is transmitted from males to females during sexual intercourse, but cannot be passed through casual contact. The FDA approved vaccine is most effective when administered during adolescence, and is only effective on females. At the time the lawsuit was brought, there was no comparable vaccine for males.

Connor Malloy, a member of the Purist Church, refuses to vaccinate her 10 year old daughter because it would violate her religion. She believes that God has a divine plan for everyone, and that it is a sin to interfere with that plan, even to protect the health of a child.

There are two parts to this exercise. In Part 1, you represent the state of Astoria and must defend the statute against a Free Exercise challenge. Jonas Barnette, another member of the Purist Church, has been deposed, and an affidavit from Dr. Rosalyn Kane has been received. Based on the testimony these witnesses could provide at trial, should you: (a) challenge the sincerity of the plaintiff's religious beliefs, (b) challenge the asserted burden on religion, or (c) concede these issues and defend the statute under the appropriate substantive standard of review? Be prepared to explain your answers.

In Part 2, you represent the challenger, Connor Malloy, and must respond to the state's summary judgment motion. At this point in the proceedings, no relevant facts are in dispute. You must therefore decide whether to challenge the merits of the statute under *Smith*, or attempt to establish that a different line of cases applies.

(Part 1) Estimated Time: Approximately 45 minutes

Task 1:   Identify facts obtained through discovery that will be useful in defending against a Free Exercise challenge.

Skill 1:   Factual development

(Part 2) Estimated Time: Approximately 1 hour

Task 2: Draft a Memorandum in Opposition to Defendant's Motion for Summary Judgment (the LexisNexis Web Course contains a form for the memorandum that has been started for you).

Skill 2: Critical reasoning

Skill 3: Motion drafting

Level of Difficulty (1 to 5):

UNITED STATES DISTRICT COURT
FOR THE DISTRICT OF ASTORIA

Connor Malloy,
    Plaintiff

v.   C.A. No. 08-5247

January 15

State of Astoria,
    Defendant

TRANSCRIBED DEPOSITION EXCERPTS

Court Reporter: Stephen Jones, RMR
    Court Reporters, Inc.
    527 Main Street
    Princeton, Astoria 52248

Plaintiff's Attorney: Stephen Maillard
    Maillard, Stern and Root, LLC
    14 North Smithfield Road
    Princeton, Astoria 52248

Defense Attorney: Kaley Samuels
    State Attorney General's Office
    224 Franklin View Parkway
    Albertson, Astoria 52241

Court Reporters, Inc.
527 Main Street
Princeton, Astoria 52248

Proceedings
(Deposition Excerpt of Jonas Barnette)

Q. Please state your name and age.

A. My name is Jonas Barnette and I am 38 years old.

Q. Tell us your address and how long you've lived there.

A. I live at 1429 Rice Lane in Acadia, and I've lived there all my life.

Q. Are you employed?

A. Well, not technically, but I spend most of my time doing things related to the church.

Q. Do you mean the Purist Church?

A. Yes, I do.

Q. For how long have you been involved with the church?

A. For the past 25 years, ever since I was 13 years old.

Q. Why did you get involved?

A. My parents started the religion on their own around the time I turned 13. We used to be Catholic, but they disagreed with many of the mainstream teachings and wanted to live by the true laws of God.

Q. How many followers belong to the Purist Church?

A. Right now we have 37 members, mostly aunts, uncles, cousins, grandparents and the like. We share the same values about God and how to live a good life on earth. A couple years ago we tried recruiting new members. We put an ad in the local paper inviting members of the community to a weekly service at my parent's house. No one showed up so I guess they're not too interested in what we're doing.

Q. What is your role in the Church as a child of the founders and now its leader?

A. Well, I lead church services and sometimes people come to me with questions about how to live a life that is pleasing to God. I try to give them good advice.

Q. So you're the church leader?

A. Well, we don't really have a leader officially. But family members come to me because I know more about what my parents thought of God than anyone else.

Q. How do you know what is "pleasing to God?" Do you look to the Bible, Quran or some other religious text?

A. No. God spoke to my parents in a series of dreams and they recorded those conversations in The Book of Purist Teachings. The advice I give is based on the Book.

Q. Does the Book of Purist Teachings say anything about child vaccinations?

A. Not expressly, no.

Q. What do you mean, not expressly?

A. God told my parents that "In the afterlife, you will be called to account for every decision you make on earth. As parents, you must not harm your children in any way, for those who do are not worthy of a life in Heaven."

Q. How does this relate to vaccinations?

A. Well, it means that parents must keep their children safe if they want to enter the kingdom of Heaven. If a vaccination can ward off a disease, then the decision not to vaccinate puts the child at harm. Parents who don't vaccinate won't go to Heaven. I was vaccinated and I don't think my parents would have done that had they thought it was against God's law.

Q. Do other members of your church believe the same thing?

A. Well, I've never talked to anyone about vaccines specifically - it's not something that's important to us one way or the other. I mean, yes, the Book says that a parent who harms a child cannot enter Heaven, and faced with a choice of giving a safe vaccine and leaving your child exposed to a disease in the future, it makes sense that you'd have to give the vaccine. But it's not something parents can't disagree on, I suppose. It doesn't mean you're kicked out of the family if you don't want to give a vaccine.

End Transcript

Dr. Rosalyn Kane
8822 State University Road, College Town, Astoria 11221;
(822) 539-7349

RE: *Connor Malloy v. State of Astoria,* Affidavit of Dr. Rosalyn Kane

I, Rosalyn Kane, under penalty of perjury, do testify and swear:

1. I am over 18 years of age and competent to testify on the matters herein set forth. I make this affidavit based on my own personal knowledge.

2. I graduated from Yale Divinity School with a Ph.D. in Comparative Religion in 1982. Between 1982 and 1985 I was a Senior Research Analyst with the United Nations Economic, Social and Cultural Organization, where I researched the position of dozens of religious organizations as it relates to medical issues and the treatment of diseases. My specific focus was on new and emerging religions that are less than 50 years old. I have been employed as a faculty member at State University since 1985 where I teach several courses on Comparative Religious Practices. I have written over 35 articles on this topic, all of which have been published in peer-reviewed journals. I belong to the Association of University Professors, the Institute for Comparative Religious Studies, and Chair the University's Committee on Religious Diversity.

3. I was asked by Attorney Kaley Samuels to provide information on the teachings of the Purist Church as they relate to physical heath issues generally and childhood vaccines in particular. Prior to Ms. Samuels' inquiry, I was not aware of the existence of the Purist Church.

4. I have sought to obtain information on the Purist Church and its teachings using generally accepted research methods, including consultation with on-line subscription databases, professional journals, and other religious studies experts. None of these sources provided information about the Purist Church.

5. No religious organization that has emerged within the past 50 years adheres to a view that it is a sin to vaccinate a child against the risk of future disease. Among the hundreds of established religions I have studied over the course of my career, only the most extreme and irrational denominations take this view. Even the Jehovah's Witnesses, known for their strong religious opposition to outside medical treatment, do not believe that it is a sin to vaccinate a child.

6. The Federal Tax Code exempts qualified charities, including religious organizations, from having to pay federal taxes. In response to Ms. Samuels' inquiry, I consulted the appropriate IRS database and found that The Purist Church is not exempt.

7. I declare under the penalty of perjury that the foregoing is true and correct to the best of my knowledge.

Dated, September 2

College Town, Astoria

Dr. Rosalyn Kane
Rosalyn Kane, Ph.D.

UNITED STATES DISTRICT COURT
FOR THE DISTRICT OF ASTORIA

Connor Malloy,

    Plaintiff

v.

State of Astoria,

    Defendant

C.A. No. 08-5247

January 15

Defendant's Motion for Summary Judgment

I. Astoria Is Not Required To Recognize A Religious Exemption From A Neutral And Generally Applicable Childhood Vaccine Requirement That Reasonably Furthers A Legitimate Health Objective

Employment Department v. Smith, 494 U.S. 872 (1990), held that the Free Exercise Clause does not require the state to exempt religious adherents from neutral, generally applicable laws. The vaccination requirement falls into this category.

Plaintiff has not alleged that the vaccine statute was enacted to burden a particular religious group. Nor could she. The statute was passed after state health officials documented a rise in cervical cancer caused by a virus that spreads through sexual intercourse. The legislature did not even know about the Purist Church until after the law was passed.

The law requires all females within the covered age group to show proof of vaccination before enrolling in school, but allows a parent who objects to the vaccination to seek an exemption by making a "good cause" showing to a designated health official. The state has granted an exemption when the vaccine would exacerbate a pre-existing medical condition, or when a doctor's office or clinic has exhausted its vaccine supply prior to the start of the school year. Purists are entitled to claim an exemption for these reasons to the same extent as any other public school students.

II. Prayer For Relief

Because the statute is a neutral, generally applicable law that furthers a legitimate health objective as described in *Smith*, its enforcement against members of the Purist Church does not violate the Free Exercise Clause. Summary judgment in favor of the Defendant is therefore appropriate.

Kevin Jones
Attorney Kevin Jones (Astoria #55497)
Assistant Attorney General
State of Astoria

**DO NOT PROCEED TO THE NEXT PAGE UNTIL YOU
HAVE COMPLETED THE EXERCISE**

SELF-ASSESSMENT

Part 1

Required Task:

Task 1: Identify facts obtained through discovery that will be useful in defending against a Free Exercise challenge.

Practice Skill Utilized:

Skill 1: Factual development

Task 1:	**Identify facts obtained through discovery that will be useful in defending against a Free Exercise challenge.**
Practice Tip:	As a junior attorney, you likely will be asked to review responses to discovery that another lawyer conducted. The task is more difficult than it first appears because there is no guarantee that discovery was conducted in a manner that would elicit legally relevant facts rather than superfluous information. Part of your job will be to identify what is *not* relevant to the case, and propose an appropriate strategy going forward. Instinct may tell you to make something out of every fact that is discovered, but a skillful attorney will not waste time, money, or resources on a lost cause.
Factual Development:	Do the facts obtained through discovery provide a basis for rebutting the plaintiff's claim that her opposition to the vaccine is based on a sincere religious belief? Think about the testimony Barnette and Kane have provided:

- The Purist Church is not a "mainstream" religion. It was started 25 years ago and still has only 37 members. It is not known to religious experts, and is not recognized as a charitable organization under the relevant tax code.

- It is not an "organized" religion. It has no organizing structure or official "leader," and may be nothing more than a group of extended family members who share similar beliefs and values.

- The "church" does not take an official position on vaccines, and at least one church member disagrees with the plaintiff's understanding of "God's law" on the issue.

- The opinion of at least one church member that the decision to withhold an anti-cancer vaccine is unreasonable, as is a parent's belief that she could not go to Heaven if she vaccinated her child.

It is unlikely that any of these facts could rebut the sincerity of the plaintiff's asserted religious belief. As stated in the introduction, whether the belief is objectively reasonable or accepted by a mainstream or organized religion is insufficient, without more, to challenge the sincerity of the plaintiff's assertion. Nor is it dispositive that the plaintiff's opposition to the vaccine differs from the original orthodoxy of her "church," if a church is indeed established. Indeed, the more a court inquires into the sincerity of the plaintiff's religious belief under the Free Exercise Clause, the more it risks entanglement with religion in violation of the Establishment Clause. Until discovery is obtained from the plaintiff herself, it will be exceedingly difficult to challenge the assertion that her opposition to childhood vaccines is grounded in religion.

SELF-ASSESSMENT

Part 2

Required Task:

Task 2: Draft a Memorandum in Opposition to Defendant's Motion for Summary Judgment.

Practice Skill Utilized:

Skill 2: Critical reasoning

Skill 3: Motion drafting

Task 2:	**Draft a Memorandum in Opposition to Defendant's Motion for Summary Judgment.**
Motion Drafting:	Refer to Skills & Values, LexisNexis Web Course, Ch. 13: Memorandum in Opposition to Defendant's Motion for Summary Judgment.
Critical Reasoning:	Astoria claims that it has enacted a neutral, generally applicable statute that is subject to rational basis review under *Smith*. But even *Smith* identified circumstances where strict scrutiny is appropriate. Does it matter that *Smith* involved a challenge to a criminal law?
	Did you consider that the "good cause" exception is available to all parents, including members of the Purist Church? Does this demonstrate the neutral, general applicability of the statute as described in *Smith*, or can you argue that it triggers heightened scrutiny review under a different line of cases?
	In addition, the statute forces parents to choose between following their religion or vaccinating their daughters so they can attend public school. Can you argue that this is a "hybrid rights" exception to the rational basis rule adopted in *Smith*? Can you rely on *Yoder*, and can you distinguish *Jacobson*?
	What arguments can you make that the statute fails to satisfy strict scrutiny?

Chapter 14
VAGUENESS AND OVERBREADTH

INTRODUCTION

In addition to the merits of a First Amendment defense, you must consider whether a law that burdens speech is susceptible to an "overbreadth" or "vagueness" challenge. These related yet distinct doctrines guard against the chilling effect that enforcement of a criminal law might have on expressive rights.

Whereas an "overbreadth" claim focuses on the scope and precision of the challenged law, "vagueness" relates to the clarity of the law. An overbroad or vague construction will render the statute void unless a constitutional construction has been provided by a court with proper jurisdiction. When the case arises in federal court, an authoritative construction of a state statute might be obtained through certification procedures, if they are available.

An overbroad statute prohibits substantially more speech than is constitutionally permissible. *Board of Airport Commissioners v. Jews for Jesus*, 482 U.S. 569 (1987). While there is no precise formula for measuring when a statute is substantially overbroad (as opposed to marginally, or merely somewhat overbroad), the analysis entails a comparison between the breadth of the challenged statute and the quantity of speech the government could permissibly regulate. For instance, whether a prohibition against "annoying or insulting comments directed to a sidewalk pedestrian" is unconstitutionally overbroad depends on how far the statute reaches beyond a permissible public forum restriction. As applied to speech in a "place of public employment," the same restriction might be overbroad if it far exceeds the bounds of a permissible non-public forum regulation.

Application of the overbreadth doctrine is "manifestly, strong medicine," because it renders a statute facially void, meaning that it cannot be applied to any defendant, even one whose speech or conduct is criminally proscribable. In practice, the doctrine would allow a defendant who engages in unconstitutional fighting words to challenge the enforcement of a "disorderly conduct" statute on the theory that other persons will refrain from engaging in protected speech for fear of being prosecuted themselves. *See Brockett v. Spokane Arcades, Inc.*, 472 U.S. 491 (1985). The doctrine effectively modifies constitutional standing requirements that typically bar an individual from asserting a claim on behalf of another person not before the court. Permitting the defendant's unprotected speech to go unpunished is considered to be less significant than the chilling effect an overbroad statute will have on protected speech.

The vagueness doctrine applies when a statute fails to meet a threshold standard of notice and definiteness. Due process dictates that a statute is vague if "persons of average intelligence must necessarily guess at its meaning and differ as to its application." *Connally v. General Construction, Co.*, 269 U.S. 385 (1926). Under this standard, an ordinance that prohibits individuals from assembling on a sidewalk and conducting themselves "in a manner annoying to persons walking by" is unconstitutionally vague because it does not provide an ascertainable standard for determining what type of proscribable conduct is "annoying." *See Coates v. Cincinnati*, 402 U.S. 611 (1971).

Particular vigilance is warranted when a statute prohibits speech because individuals may hesitate to engage in constitutionally protected expression for fear of violating an indecipherable law. Drafting precision also provides guidance to law enforcement officers and guards against the risk that a statute will be selectively enforced against an unpopular speaker.

Practice Tip: Criminal statutes often include a "severability clause" to signal the lawmakers' intent that part of a statute remain in effect if any other part is found unconstitutional. This is one way of preserving the integrity of a broad statutory scheme when one particular aspect of the scheme is rendered invalid.

Exercise 14:

You are a criminal defense attorney in Massachusetts whose clients are charged with having violated various state code provisions and municipal ordinances. In addition to defending each case on the merits, you also plan to assert an overbreadth or vagueness challenge where appropriate.

The information below indicates the procedural posture of each client's case, the relevant statute or ordinance, and the preliminary results of research you have conducted thus far. Indicate in each circumstance whether an overbreadth or vagueness challenge is likely to succeed.

Required Tasks:

Task 1: Determine whether the law in question is substantially overbroad or impermissibly vague.

Task 2: Revise the statute or ordinance so that it is more likely to withstand a constitutional attack (the LexisNexis Web Course contains an editable version of each statute or ordinance).

Practice Skill Utilized:

Skill 1: Critical analysis

Skill 2: Legislative drafting

Estimated Time for Completion: Approximately 45 minutes

Level of Difficulty (1 to 5):

Case 1: Your client is charged with violating an ordinance that bans "three or more persons from assembling on a sidewalk in a manner intended to annoy others." Charges are brought in state court.

You determine that:

- The ordinance is intended to discourage illegal gang activity.
- The ordinance has not been narrowed by any construction of the state's highest court, the Massachusetts Supreme Judicial Court.
- *Coates v. Cincinnati*, 402 U.S. 611 (1971), invalidated a similar statute on vagueness grounds because it provided no ascertainable standard of conduct by which an average person could determine what was prohibited.

Could you successfully assert a vagueness challenge?

Could you successfully assert an overbreadth challenge?

Case 2: Your client is charged with violating a state statute that prohibits "the sale or distribution of any material that is obscene." Charges are pending in state court.

You determine that:

- The statute has not been narrowed by any construction of the state supreme court.
- *Board of Airport Commissioners of the City of Los Angeles v. Jews for Jesus, Inc.*, 482 U.S. 569 (1987), invalidated a statute that prohibited "all First Amendment activities" in the Los Angeles airport as substantially overbroad.

Can you successfully assert a vagueness challenge?

Can you successfully assert an overbreadth challenge?

Case 3: A city ordinance prohibits juveniles from "perusing" city streets between the hours of 7:00 a.m. and 3:00 p.m. "Perusing" is defined as "placing one's self on a city street without a clear objective." Your client is arrested and charged with violating the ordinance.

Before trial, you discover that:

- The ordinance is intended to curb juvenile truancy and loitering.
- In a previous case, the Massachusetts Supreme Court concluded that the ordinance was unconstitutionally vague because it gave police officers absolute discretion to determine what activities constitute "perusing."
- You file a motion to dismiss, and charges against your client are dropped. You then file a civil rights action against the arresting officer in federal court alleging unlawful arrest. As a defense, the officer's attorney argues that the arrest was not unlawful because the ordinance is susceptible to a more limited constitutional construction than that given by the Massachusetts Supreme Court. How do you respond?

DO NOT PROCEED TO THE NEXT PAGE UNTIL YOU HAVE COMPLETED THE EXERCISE

SELF-ASSESSMENT

Case 1: You client is charged with violating an ordinance that bans "three or more persons from assembling on a sidewalk in a manner intended to annoy others." Charges are brought in state court.

You determine that:

- The ordinance is intended to discourage illegal gang activity.
- The ordinance has not been narrowed by any construction of the state's highest court, the Massachusetts Supreme Judicial Court.

Coates v. Cincinnati, 402 U.S. 611 (1971), invalidated a similar statute on vagueness grounds because it provided no ascertainable standard of conduct by which an average person could determine what was prohibited.

Could you successfully assert an overbreadth challenge?

Could you successfully assert a vagueness challenge?

Critical Analysis: Vagueness: Yes, you might succeed in a vagueness challenge, but be cautious about relying too much on *Coates*. That case may serve as persuasive authority because the ordinance under review, like the ordinance here, had not been constitutionally narrowed by an appropriate state court, and the Supreme Court found that it was not susceptible to a limiting instruction. However, in your case, the drafting history behind the ordinance may justify a narrowing construction, unlike the ordinance in *Coates*. If so, the facts will determine whether your client can still be charged.

Overbreadth: Yes, the ordinance might also be substantially overbroad. Compare the potential reach of the statute with the kinds of speech or speech related conduct that could be prohibited. Is the difference substantial enough to render the ordinance facially invalid?

Legislative Drafting: Refer to Skills & Values Chapter 14, LexisNexis Web Course: Draft Legislation

Case 2: Your client is charged with violating a state statute that prohibits "the sale or distribution of any material that is obscene." Charges are pending in state court.

You determine that:

- The statute has not been narrowed by any construction of the state supreme court.
- *Board of Airport Commissioners of the City of Los Angeles v. Jews for Jesus, Inc.*, 482 U.S. 569 (1987), invalidated a statute that prohibited "all First Amendment activities" in the Los Angeles airport as substantially overbroad.

Can you successfully assert an overbreadth challenge?

Can you successfully assert a vagueness challenge?

Critical Analysis: Overbreadth: The regulation in *Jews for Jesus* prohibited all forms of protected expression pursuant to language that was not susceptible to a limiting instruction. A statute that bans the sale or distribution of "obscene" material applies only to unprotected speech. Unlike a prohibition on "all First Amendment activities," the ban on obscenity is not substantially overbroad because it applies to speech the state already has the authority to prohibit.

Vagueness: The state statute might be unconstitutionally vague, however. A properly drawn obscenity statute must reference "specifically defined sex acts." This statute fails to meet that requirement and in doing so, might be challenged on the merits, as well as on the grounds that it does not provide reasonable notice as to the type of material that is prohibited. Nor does it provide sufficient standards for curbing law enforcement discretion.

Legislative Drafting: Refer to Skills & Values Chapter 14, LexisNexis Web Course: Draft Legislation

Case 3: A city ordinance prohibits juveniles from "perusing" city streets between the hours of 7:00 am and 3:00 pm. "Perusing" is defined as "placing one's self on a city street without a clear objective." Your client is arrested and charged with violating the ordinance.

Before trial, you discover that:

- The ordinance is intended to curb juvenile truancy and loitering.
- In a previous case, the Massachusetts Supreme Court concluded that the ordinance was unconstitutionally vague because it gave police officers absolute discretion to determine what activities constitute "perusing."

You file a motion to dismiss, and charges against your client are dropped. You then file a civil rights action against the arresting officer in federal court alleging unlawful arrest. As a defense, the officer's attorney argues that the arrest was not unlawful because the ordinance is susceptible to a more limited constitutional construction than that given by the Massachusetts Supreme Court. How do you respond?

Critical Analysis: Vagueness: A federal court is bound by the authoritative construction given to a statute or ordinance by an appropriate state court. It cannot "re-interpret" a statute or ordinance once it has been construed. *See Chicago v. Morales*, 527 U.S. 41 (1999).

Legislative Drafting: Refer to Skills & Values Chapter 14, LexisNexis Web Course: Draft Legislation